THE MIGHTY MOUTH

Presented to: _____

On: _____

Message: _____

_____

_____

_____

_____

_____

_____

_____

_____

_____

_____

Presented by: _____

THE
MIGHTY
MOUTH

Jeani McKeever-Harroun

THE MIGHTY MOUTH

Printed in the United States of America
First printing August, 2000

Omega Publications
P. O. Box 4130
Medford, Oregon 97501
U.S.A.

ISBN #0-86694-154-1 (Softback)

This book is available at quantity discounts for bulk purchases. For information, call 800-343-1111

Visit our home page at:
http://omegapublications.com

TABLE OF CONTENTS

DETAILED OUTLINE

FOREWORD

By Jack Harroun

Sometimes there are situations wherein we get stuck emotionally. We can find ourselves carrying anger toward a person or about something that has happened, perhaps feeling resentful about certain facts in our life. We know we don't like it and we don't want to be there, but we don't know how to change things.

It was my privilege to help Jeani edit this book. During the times we went through it, I found myself internalizing some of the principles that I had either forgotten or had yet to learn and apply in my spiritual training. The effects impacted me subconsciously, as well as consciously. Even on the golf course, I viewed the game and my opponents differently. The importance of this message was reinforced when I realized that the book was indeed what the Hawaiians term "ke ala pono"—the right path.

Recently, my golfing partner, fifteen years my senior, afforded me the safe haven to vent, concerning some anger I was holding inside in regard to a certain individual. After working on this manuscript with Jeani, I was amazed at the care with which I shared my frustrations with him. I truly didn't want to cast any negative aspersions because of the possibilities of spiritual ramifications.

Likewise with an engine I recently purchased that was assured to be in excellent condition. It did not live up to that which was promised and I was livid. Unfortunately, I've been known to roar like a thousand lions. But as a result of having the spiritual laws from this book fresh in my mind, the awareness that God would balance the scales in His time was overwhelming. Consequently, I was able to guard my words and leave the resolution in His hand.

Many times, life situations require preparation. Right behaviors and speech need to be rehearsed. This book is a valuable tool to aid in that preparation. It highlights spiritual laws to live by that unlock a correctness of thought and behavior. Among the gifts of this book that I received was the necessity and importance of forgiveness and an avenue to accomplish that. It also provides guidelines as to how to avoid creating unnecessary relational wreckage. There is a gentle knowing of what is right that falls over the reader, like a new-found discipline. This book can help you be the kind of person you want to be.

QUOTES

"At Babel, human speech became the source of confusion; at Pentecost human speech became the instrument of clarity which God chose to spread the message of His salvation to all people."[1]
—Ron Williams

"As an attorney I was trained to use my tongue to win, to defend, to be negative and critical. Jeani's book gives a tremendous spiritual direction, as well as a personal and down-to-earth illustration of the things one's mouth can do positively as well as negatively. Christ is the one who can help us in the manner in which we use our words to build up and affirm."
—Roger L. Minor, Attorney

"Such an important message for 21st century Christians! Most of us don't think much about what we say. We really need this."
—Dr. June Breninger, Professor of Psychology

"This book carries an eternal message for all, regardless of age, maturity, sex or religious background. According to the Bible, the one who speaks perfectly is perfect (James 3:2)....And none of us is there yet! Therefore, we will always have room for improvement and a need to revisit this primary, essential, foundational issue of the heart."
—Pastor Lee Korner, Central Point Christian Fellowship

"A lot of things came together for me from the Bible in reading this. I love this book!"
—Debbie Horton

"A very positive, clearly-written message. I was very pleased to see that this was a practical, sensible book that can be of benefit to those from all faiths."
—Nancy Spillman

"We have all been hurt and helped by the words of others. This book brings to light the power that is

available in the words we speak to one another.   'The Mighty Mouth' serves as a good reminder to each of us, to be conscious and aware of what comes out of our mouth."
                                                    —*Shone Ellis*

"This is a truly wonderful and inspiring message by a gifted communicator.   Jeani's words help to focus the readers' heart and thoughts on God's glory and the power of words to hurt or to heal.   She integrates personal insights with scriptural quotes in a seamless way that makes the text very easy to follow.   A good book for just about anybody!"   —*Laurel Kinnear*

"A great reminder of the power behind the words we speak...both good and bad. Jeani's book is a good balance of personal experience, practical application and Scripture to back up what she says.   It caused me to reflect on things said in the past and how I want to say things in the future.
"I didn't realize when I sat down to read this how much I needed to read it.   When my temper gets ignited, I say things I regret later.   This book is right on!   It hit a chord with me.   Everyone should read it!"
                                                    —*Barbara Minor*

"Excellent!   Right on!   This shows how much of our life revolves around our words."   —*Shelley Kristen Trickel*

"I pray that this book will convict others and cause them to reflect on their words and how they speak them, as it did for   me."
                                                    —*Becky Otto*

"God spoke, and the universe sprang into existence. Then He made man in His image and imbued our words with a measure of creative power as well. 'The Mighty Mouth' explores the depth of this power, and reveals how it can be used to edify the body of Christ and increase the effectiveness of the individual Christian. This book is must reading for any person committed to following in the footsteps of Jesus."
                                                    —*Jim Andrews*

ACKNOWLEDGEMENTS

My hat is off to my terrific secretary, Shone Ellis, for her tireless patience in typesetting and working in book corrections around our regular workload and deadlines.

A heart-felt thank you goes to those who freely gave the gift of their time to review this manuscript prior to publication and responded with invaluable feedback:

Jack Harroun
Jim Andrews
Dr. June Breninger
Debbie Horton
Laurel Kinnear
Lee Korner
Roger & Barbara Minor
Becky Otto
Nancy Spillman
Shelley Kristen Trickel

I especially appreciate the creative editorial comments of my darling husband, Jack, who temporarily laid aside work on his own manuscript to help me improve this one and finish it up for press. His support and timely collaboration definitely strengthened this work. He's the wind beneath my wings.

Above all, I'm grateful to the Lord for lessons learned and the opportunity to offer this to you. I pray that perspectives shared may bring a glimpse of enlightenment to other truth seekers.

*For we all often stumble and fall
and offend in many things.
And if any one does not offend in speech—
never says the wrong things—
he is a fully developed character and a perfect man,
able to control his whole body
and to curb his entire nature.*

—*James 3:2, Amplified*

PREFACE

The Scriptures have so much more to say on the power of the tongue than I have addressed in these pages. The concepts herein are drawn from a much longer study I have outlined on this fascinating and pertinent subject. However, enough is examined here to introduce to you the importance of the words we speak in the eyes of the Lord and in the effect they have on our relationships.

Another upcoming book in progress is entitled *Christian Warriors—Spiritual Preparedness*. The constructive use of our words would comprise just one chapter of that multifaceted book—that is to say that the words we speak are one *potentially very powerful weapon in our spiritual arsenal*. It is my belief that this is a weapon all-too-often misused or largely ignored in its life-giving significance. That is why I have chosen initially to publish this treatise in an abbreviated form. It's a subject that well deserves to be heeded and applied. So doing can have revolutionary positive consequences in our lives and how we relate to others.

It is my wish that the thoughts in these pages will inspire you to consider more carefully what flows out of your mouth and the effect it can have on people, both for good or ill. Within you resides the ability to impart *words of life* that will uplift another. It is my prayer that a desire will be unleashed in you to let the words of your mouth and the meditation of your heart be acceptable in His sight (Ps. 19:14) and to utilize this divine tool for the immeasurable good that is available to you.

Let the words of my mouth
and the meditation of my heart
be acceptable in Thy sight,
O LORD, my rock and my redeemer.

—Psalm 19:14

chapter 1

THE POWER
OF THE TONGUE

*"In the beginning was the Word, and the
Word was with God, and the Word was God."*
                                        —*John 1:1*

Picture a baby reaching the age where he is pulling
himself up on furniture and learning to hold his weight on
his legs, tottering towards taking his first step. Mom and
dad are crouched three feet away, arms outstretched
saying, "Come on, Honey! You can do it!" They are
smiling and encouraging, vocalizing his praise, as he
teeteringly takes one, then two, wavering steps in their
direction before plunging headlong into their waiting arms.

It goes without saying that parental encouragement
has much to do with the building of a child's confidence
that he can take those first steps. And these are just the
beginning of many "first steps" in life where a parent's
input is significant.

Virginia Satire is loosely quoted as having said, *"It's
impossible to fully know how our words and actions
impact our children."*

I am reminded of the movie *Quarterback Princess*, based on the true story of a Canadian girl who wanted to play high school football. Fortunately, she had parents who believed in her and told her she could do anything to which she applied herself. They supported her dreams and her goals verbally and actively. Not only did she go on to play with the high school football team, but she became the winning quarterback! If that were not enough, she also was elected homecoming queen at the end of the year.

My point is this: Our verbal support of people in our lives can have a tremendous impact on their belief system about what they can and cannot do.

In contrast, consider this example. On one of his tapes, Paul Hegstrom, Founder of Life Skills International, cites a painful childhood memory from a time when he was looking to his mother for encouragement, healing and some understanding.[1] A bewildering violation had just occurred. At nine years of age, he was sexually molested and he apprehensively tried to share this offense with her. To test the waters, he disguised the trauma with a third person example. Instead of receiving words of safety and reassurance, the verbal messages he heard from his unsuspecting mother were that any child that happened to was *dirty, damaged* and *different*. As you might imagine, those verbal judgments resounded deeply in his young psyche and further compounded the profoundly damaging effect of the sexual abuse. It was twenty-nine years later before Paul began to find a path of healing, true recovery and restoration.[2] Chances are that if his mother had known the truth about her sons' story, her message to him would have been very different at that critical moment.

Truly our words have an impact far greater than we may realize.

THE SIGNIFICANCE OF OUR WORDS

"Death and life are in the power of the tongue..."

—*Proverbs 18:21a*

There is a profusion of passages interwoven throughout the Scriptures concerning the theme of *our words* and their significance. We wield tremendous power with the spoken word, whether or not we are aware of it. With our mouths we can curse, inflict pain and injury, accuse and condemn. Or, with those same lips, we can bless and implant peace, joy, and hope in place of despair or hopelessness. With the tongue we can speak life or death. We can edify another human being or, just as easily, we can devastate and tear down. It's our choice.

Genesis relates that God created the world by His word. He *spoke* things into being. His words were creative and life-giving, with incredible power:

3   Then God said, "Let there be light;" and there was light.

—Genesis 1

The Psalmist said: *"by the word of the Lord the heavens were made...He spoke and it was done"* (see Ps. 33:6, 9).

In the book of John, we read the following—familiar words to many—in reference to Jesus:

1   In the beginning was the Word, and the Word was with God, and the Word was God.
2   He was in the beginning with God.

3 All things came into being by Him, and apart from Him nothing came into being that has come into being.

—John 1

All things came into being through the creative *Word* of God. God's word had, and still has, incredible power. And we are also told in the Scriptures that *man is made in God's image* (Gen. 1:26, 27).

HOW IS MAN DIFFERENT?

One of the main things that distinguishes man from other animals is *speech*. Certain species walk upright. Chimpanzees have intelligence and manual dexterity and can be trained to do many things that man does. Animals can rebel; they can exhibit emotion. But man alone is endowed with the ability to speak in words, to express himself verbally. For one thing, this allows mankind to pass on detailed knowledge from one generation to the next.

One result of being made in God's image is that *our words carry an immense power—power to a degree far beyond that which I believe many of us have fully grasped.*

Given that we have this special gift of speech, how are we going to utilize this most amazing faculty? Will we choose to use our speech to edify and speak life instead of in destructive or hurtful ways? I believe that the wise use of our words is very important and often-overlooked tool at our disposal.

POWER TO TEAR DOWN OR BUILD UP

The book of James contains one of the most enlightening passages in Scripture on the power of the tongue. Because it is so poetically descriptive, let's read it in its entirety.

2 For we all stumble in many *ways*. If anyone does not stumble in what he says he is a perfect man, able to bridle the whole body as well.

3 Now if we put the bits into the horses' mouths so that they may obey us, we direct their entire body as well.

4 Behold, the ships also, though they are so great and are driven by strong winds, are still directed by a very small rudder, wherever the inclination of the pilot desires.

5 So also the tongue is a small part of the body, and *yet* it boasts of great things.

6 And the tongue is a fire, the *very* world of iniquity; the tongue is set among our members as that which defiles the entire body, and sets on fire the course of *our* life, and is set on fire by hell.

7 For every species of beasts and birds, of reptiles and creatures of the sea, is tamed, and has been tamed by the human race.

8 But no one can tame the tongue; *it is* a restless evil *and* full of deadly poison.

9 With it we bless *our* Lord and Father; and with it we curse men, who have been made in the likeness of God;

10 from the same mouth come *both* blessing and cursing. My brethren, these things ought not to be this way.

—James 3

James uses the very descriptive analogy of a horse's bit (vs. 3). A small piece of metal in a horse's mouth, perhaps 6 inches wide, can be used to direct and control the power of a mighty 1200-pound animal! Likewise, a huge ship can be steered by a small rudder in the water, according to the inclination of the captain. Since the course heading is determined by the rudder, the ship's destination can shift drastically if the rudder is off just a few degrees! Much like a ship's rudder, the use of our tongue can determine our life's journey and destination, as well as significantly impact the voyage of others. James uses these illustrations as graphic examples of how one in control of his tongue truly is master over his entire body (vs. 2).

In verse 10, James aptly states that from the same mouth can come both blessing and cursing. As the preceding passage clearly reveals, the tongue can be "full of deadly poison." With just a few words we can destroy the reputation of another. A husband can crush his wife emotionally with an unkind or demeaning remark. A wife can likewise totally demoralize her husband by a statement of scorn and ridicule instead of one of understanding and support.

In the next two verses, the writer goes on to question:

11 Does a fountain send out from the same opening *both* fresh and bitter *water*?

12 Can a fig tree, my brethren, produce olives, or a vine produce figs? Neither *can* salt water produce fresh.

—James 3

The implication is that if evil or hurtful words are coming out of our mouth, we would do well to ponder what is poisoning our water—that is, our inner self. By and large, it is an indication that there is something causing internal pain or distress that needs to be examined. Later, we will discuss further the connection between what is in our heart and the words that come out of our mouth.

The import of our words is of major significance in the development of character and spiritual maturity. Therefore, it is absolutely essential that we control our speech.

Proverbs states that our words can even bring healing.

18 There is one who speaks rashly like the thrusts of a sword,
But the tongue of the wise brings healing.
—Proverbs 12

A word of encouragement spoken to someone in a time of despair or deep disillusionment can serve as a lighthouse of hope, a beacon of truth that he or she can lock onto to get through one of life's storms. Never underestimate the power of such a word. The Holy Spirit can breathe life into it and turn somebody around.

One of Winston Churchill's most famous speeches took place in possibly England's darkest hour during World War II. He was given a lengthy introduction and everyone was anxiously awaiting the words of this highly-respected Prime Minister. Finally, the podium was relinquished. After carefully observing his audience for some time, Churchill gave perhaps the world's shortest speech. He said:

"NEVER, NEVER, NEVER, *NEVER,* **NEVER** GIVE UP."

He then sat down. Powerful, timely words, spoken with authority and conviction that gave hope to a nation, perhaps the saving hope.

Words, timely spoken, are one of the tools our Lord uses. Something *you* say to someone may be just the anchor that person needs in a given moment.

The Scriptures are replete with references that support what is said in the book of James. I will quote quite a number through the course of these pages to give you the flavor of how very important this subject is to God. There are many, many more verses that could be used as well. (It is a fascinating and eye-opening study to research *all* that the Bible has to say about this subject.)

The wise King Solomon offered much instruction and insight about our words in his frequent references to them in the book of Proverbs. Here are a few that speak volumes of truth:

> **11 The mouth of the righteous is a fountain of life,**
> **But the mouth of the wicked conceals violence....**
> **14 Wise men store up knowledge,**
> **But with the mouth of the foolish, ruin is at**
> **hand....**
>
> **18 He who conceals hatred *has* lying lips,**
> **And he who spreads slander is a fool.**
> **19 When there are many words, transgression is**
> **unavoidable,**
> **But he who restrains his lips is wise,**
> **20 The tongue of the righteous is *as* choice silver,...**
> **21 The lips of the righteous feed many,...**
> **—Proverbs 10**

If you read this passage carefully, you will see that Solomon has much wisdom to share about the power we wield with our tongue. Here are several more verses. Note here that there is *fruit* from what we speak:

> **2 From the fruit of a man's mouth he enjoys good,...**
> **17 A wicked messenger falls into adversity, But a faithful envoy brings healing.**
> **—Proverbs 13**
>
> **11 By blessing of the upright a city is exalted, But by the mouth of the wicked it is torn down.**
> **—Proverbs 11**

We give evil a foothold when we are unnecessarily critical. Inane criticism without purpose can be a breeding ground for all sorts of evil. We do well to watch critical judgments that come out of our mouths.

JOHN AND BETTY'S MIRACLE

I once read an article about a couple, whom I will call John and Betty, who experienced an interesting transformation in their marriage. Betty used to nag John unmercifully. No matter what he did, it seemed she only pointed out what was wrong. Eventually he began to work later at the office to delay coming home to an inevitable barrage of complaints, problems and negative thinking. Pretty soon, he frequently was finding excuses to work late into the evenings and he found lots of things that he had to do on the weekends with his buddies.

Mind you, John was no more accomplished than Betty, as far as what came out of his mouth. There was no end to what he found wrong with the way she did things. He commented regularly that she was a lousy housekeeper, a slob, and that she did not live up to his expectations as a wife and mother.

Then one day when John came home, instead of being greeted with a hostile comment or some accusing remark, his wife kissed him warmly and told him, in a most genuine tone, how glad she was to see him. The rest of the evening progressed without any of the typical bickering from her. Even when he chided her about the dust she had missed on the top of the refrigerator and his unpressed shirts, she remained uncharacteristically unflappable. In fact, to his surprise, she responded sympathetically with an apology that she had been unable to get to those things during the day, but she would be sure to do them the next day while he was at work.

Intrigued by this baffling new air about his wife, John could hardly wait to get home the following day. Again he was greeted warmly at the door. He discovered that—sure enough—his work shirts had been pressed and hung neatly in the closet. The house was well kept and he found himself at a loss for any of his habitual nasty and demeaning comments. Instead, the couple chatted frankly over a lovely dinner his wife had prepared and she showed a genuine interest in what he had to share about his challenges at work. By the end of the evening, he was quite refreshed and thoroughly enjoying the company of his wife, as though he were getting to know a brand new person.

The next day, John was eager to get home again. He even made an excuse to leave work a few minutes early so he could go and be with his wife. This day she had something legitimate to complain about—he had not emptied the boxes of trash he had cleared out of his shop, as he said he would. As a result, she had been unable to clean the porch. However, instead of barking, as she once would have done, she gently reminded him about the trash, saying she understood that he had been busy with work and that it probably had just slipped his mind. She then volunteered to help him attend to the task.

Quite overwhelmed, he gladly agreed, and they cleared away the garbage together. All the while, John kept apologizing that he had been shirking his duties and responsibilities around the house and leaving all of the household chores to her. He even offered to help her with the dishes after dinner—something he had never done in all their years of married life. As they worked together, he asked her about her day, finding himself truly interested in what she had been doing and her perspective on things.

Betty just beamed. She found herself falling in love with her husband all over again, wanting to spend more time with him and eager to go out of her way to do things to please him.

Before long, even the children began to comment on the change in both of them. They were spending much more time together as a family and enjoying every minute of it. Friends who came to visit noticed a new closeness and the loving way they spoke of each other. The absence of harsh and critical words was very evident and it made this couple much more enjoyable to be around.

You might be wondering what caused this change. Betty had heard a speaker challenge the listeners to do away with negative, critical speech and to concentrate on making constructive, uplifting comments instead. In that moment, she realized she was missing the love and respect of her husband and the family harmony she would like to have. She resolved that she would guard her tongue and watch her words for a week. The decision she had made had been a hard one to implement, but she was finding it much easier with each new day. That week soon grew to be a month. The new-found kindness that she was seeing in her husband was an unexpected reward that helped her to be strong in her resolve to watch carefully all the words that she was speaking and to do away with negative, unedifying speech.

Although there were other dynamics at work in the situation as well, the point of this story is the power of words that are spoken in kindness. It may not always work out with the dramatic results experienced by John and Betty. However, the likelihood of some good fruit following one's efforts is high. Something as simple as a decision made by one individual to guard his or her words and to speak that which is edifying can turn a marriage around or be a healing balm in any kind of relationship.

A MYTH ABOUT WORDS

I would like to eradicate a well-known myth many of us have heard in the form of a childhood rhyme:

"Sticks and stones may break my bones, but words can never hurt me."

They lie. The truth is that words can, in fact, hurt very deeply. While it is true that we have a choice of how we respond to what we hear, an unkind word, once spoken, can be very damaging and can produce life-long wounds. It is much easier to be careful with the words that we speak in the first place, than to try to take back something that we have said in haste or in an angry outburst that has wounded another individual emotionally.

The poet expressed it well in this verse:

Boys flying kites haul in their white-winged birds;
You can't do that way when you're flying words.[3]

—*Will M. Carleton*

Undoubtedly, we all have had the experience of receiving a phone call or having a verbal interaction with someone from which we came away feeling emotionally upset. It may even be a small thing that was said, but unsettling words can make it difficult to concentrate on our work or other responsibilities. Much inner turmoil can be fueled by just a few ill-spoken words.

Conversely, a few well-chosen and timely words of encouragement or cheer can do much to make someone's day. The choice is ours: *Will we use our words to tear down and bring confusion, pain and misery to others, or to edify, encourage and support?*

A negative comment like, "You'll never amount to anything," or, "You will never be able to do that" by a parent, a sibling or someone in authority can influence the life of a child forever. It can be like a "life command" deposited into the heart that subconsciously stays with him throughout his life. Through this marred filter the child's view of himself (his self-image) is formed.

Imagine a parent saying to a child regularly, "You're good for nothing! You are always getting into some kind of trouble!" How do you think that child will continue to behave? Very likely he will continue to get into trouble, because that is the programming that has been fed into his mental computer. It becomes a self-fulfilling prophecy.

I am extremely grateful for the edifying deposits of encouraging words made into my life over the years by those who believed in me, like my mother, my father, my husband, certain friends and special teachers. I can think back of those who kindly looked beyond my obvious weak areas and limitations and saw instead my potential. They used the incredibly-powerful gift of supportive words to *inspire* me to believe in myself, to believe that I had something worthwhile to contribute. Their positive, edifying words are partly responsible for any good whatsoever that may have come of my life.

A number of years ago, I had the privilege of recording two music tapes. I recognize that I am no Julie Andrews—nor do I have illusions that I ever will be—but I do have a passion for worship and music. I knew at the time that these simple tapes would never sell a million, yet it was something on my heart to do. In regard to this, I thank God that I was fortunate to have parents who had encouraged me to be the best that I could be musically, as well as in other areas of interest. I'm also particularly grateful for the words of encouragement from my late husband, James McKeever, and others along the way who helped build my confidence that I had something worthwhile to contribute, even though I lacked the expertise and refining of professional vocal training.

I distinctly remember once receiving a disheartening letter from a lady—most likely a trained musician herself—who returned one of my music tapes with some very negative comments. My feelings were hurt, not because she returned the tape, but in response to her unconstructively critical words. My husband, Jack, a trained musician and singer himself, tells me that I'm just thin-skinned and that any professional musician soon learns not to take criticism of any kind to heart, but to simply learn and grow from it. I will not deny the veracity of this. Maybe it's simply a character weakness, but this I do know: I am personally much more motivated to live up to my potential by *constructive* criticism and encouragement than by someone telling me I *can't* do something. For me, that kind of input serves only to erode any desire or will to try.

The good news is that, just as negative input can hinder and become a self-fulfilling prophecy, positive input can *inspire* and help eradicate the damaging effects of past negative words. *Never, never* underestimate the impact that your words can have upon another person.

A good question to ask yourself as a guide for your words is this: Do they bring life and are they motivated by love?

Our words are powerful weapons. Let's be careful how we wield them.

You are a *mighty mouth.*

Chapter 2

WE REAP WHAT WE SOW

Undoubtedly you are familiar with the well-used phrase, "we reap what we sow." It is paraphrased from a verse in the Bible that says, *"whatever a man sows, this he will also reap"* (Gal. 6:7).

This is validated by the agricultural profession. If a farmer plants wheat seeds, he is going to reap *wheat*, not rye or oats. Seeds from an apple will produce more apples, not oranges, lemons or pears. Likewise with the words of our mouth: if we sow good words, we will reap good, whereas evil words can only bring evil back upon us.

> 14 **A man will be satisfied with good by the fruit of his words,**
>   **And the deeds of a man's hands will return to him....**
> 19 **Truthful lips will be established forever,**
>   **But a lying tongue is only for a moment....**
> 25 **Anxiety in the heart of a man weighs it down,**
>   **But a good word makes it glad.**
>
> **—Proverbs 12**

With our words, as well as our deeds, we reap what we sow. As we just read, a good word makes the heart

glad. If we speak good words, we will receive good fruit
in return. A spiritual principle is involved here.

The prophet Hosea speaks of *"the fruit of lies,"* an
undesirable consequence of having a lying tongue:

> **12 Sow with a view to righteousness,**
> **Reap in accordance with kindness;**
> **Break up your fallow ground,**
> **For it is time to seek the LORD**
> **Until He comes to rain righteousness on you.**
> **13 You have plowed wickedness, you have reaped**
> **injustice,**
> **You have eaten the fruit of lies.**
>
> **—Hosea 10**

Those who plow and sow wickedness, reap injustice
and will eat the fruit of their lies. One possible definition
of "the *fruit* of lies" would be false beliefs leading to
negative consequences or outcomes. Rather, we want the
words we speak to be sown in kindness, with a view to
righteousness.

Jesus Himself poetically discussed the fact that we
will reap what we sow when He spoke these poignant,
life-changing words:

> **1 "Do not judge lest you be judged *yourselves.***
> **2 "For in the way you judge, you will be judged;**
> **and by your standard of measure, it shall be measured**
> **to you."**
>
> **—Matthew 7**

The Amplified Bible gives further illumination as to
the meaning of these verses:

> **1 Do not judge *and* criticize *and* condemn others,**
> **so that you may not be judged *and* criticized *and***
> **condemned yourselves.**

2 For just as you judge *and* criticize *and* condemn others you will be judged *and* criticized *and* condemned, and in accordance with the measure you deal out to others it will be dealt out again to you.
—Matthew 7, *Amplified*

In short, the same way we treat others, we will be treated. If it be with judgment, criticism and condemnation, we can expect to receive the same back. As Rick Joyner aptly puts it, if we want to receive grace, we had better start sowing grace![1]

Proverbs warns us that our words can be a snare to us, meaning that we can be entrapped by the consequences of what we have spoken. This is yet another way of stating that we will reap what we have sown with our words:

**13 An evil man is ensnared by the transgression of his lips,
But the righteous will escape from trouble.**
—Proverbs 12

There are also numerous references that let us know loudly and clearly that God does not look kindly upon lies.

GOD HATES LIES

One of the things the Bible explicitly tells us that the Lord hates is a lying tongue:

**16 There are six things which the Lord hates,
Yes, seven which are an abomination to Him:
17 Haughty eyes, a lying tongue,
And hands that shed innocent blood,
18 A heart that devises wicked plans,**

>   Feet that run rapidly to evil,
> 19 A false witness who utters lies,
>   And one who spreads strife among brothers.
>   —Proverbs 6

Did you notice the *three* of the *seven* things listed here that the Lord hates have to do with *our words*? He hates:

1. A lying tongue (verse 17)
2. A false witness who utters lies (verse 19)
3. One who spreads strife among brothers (verse 19)

How is strife spread? Generally it involves words, in some way. The unity of His body is important to God and He does not take kindly to those who would spread contention and strife among the brothers.

The Scriptures make it clear that we can sin (miss the mark) with our mouth, intimating that curses and lies fall into this category:

> 12 *On account of* the sin of their mouth *and* the
>   words of their lips,
>   Let them even be caught in their pride,
>   And on account of curses and lies which they
>   utter.
>   —Psalm 59

Interestingly, our lies have a way of coming back to haunt us and reaping their own recompense. The story comes to mind of the little boy whose mother had set out a bowl of peanuts for a bridge game and instructed him, "Don't touch the peanuts." Being a typical little boy, he was sorely tempted by the appealing bowl of peanuts. He thought, "Well, if I just take one, nobody will notice." So he took one and sure enough you couldn't even tell. Then he thought, "Well, if I just take a couple more, nobody will be able to tell." So he did, and you can imagine how this proceeded. Pretty soon he had taken so many that you really *could* notice the difference. His mother came in and said, "Have you been eating the peanuts?" He said, "No," but the evidence of his lie was undeniably apparent to his mother.

Along a similar line, a pastor who used to live in the valley here tells the story of how, as a young boy, he cleverly devised a way to stack the chocolate chip cookies in the jar so that the quantity in the container appeared the same, even after he had eaten a number. His mother entered the kitchen, looked in the cookie jar and stated, "You've been into the cookies!" Flabbergasted at being discovered, he asked, "How did you know?" She said, "Your mouth gave you away—it has chocolate chip cookie crumbs all over it!"

Yes, one way or another, our mouth will give us away when we least expect it.

WHERE DO LIES ORIGINATE?

Isaiah indicates that lying words are conceived and uttered from the heart:

> 13 ...Conceiving *in* and uttering from the heart lying words.
>
> —Isaiah 59

Much more could be said about the significance of our heart attitude and its effect on our words. No wonder the Scriptures exhort us to watch over our heart with all diligence, for from it flow the very springs of life (Prov. 4:20).

WORDS AS WEAPONS

It is important to realize that we can use our words as *weapons* for either good *or* evil. They are that powerful! Psalms speaks of men with tongues that are as *"a sharp sword,"* who breathe forth fire:

> **4 My soul is among lions;**
> **I must lie among those who breathe forth fire,**
> **_Even_ the sons of men, whose teeth are spears**
> **and arrows,**
> **And their tongue a sharp sword.**
>
> **—Psalm 57**

In Psalm 64, David prays to be hidden from the counsel of evildoers who *"have sharpened their tongue as a sword"* and *"have aimed bitter speech as their arrow"* (vs. 2-4). He also refers to the deceitful and destructive tongue of his enemy as being *"like a sharp razor"* that devours (Ps. 52:2-4). Ouch!

Toward the completion of this manuscript, I ran across an excellent article written by Rabbi Joseph Telushkin entitled "Words That Hurt, Words That Heal: How To Choose Words Wisely And Well." He made these interesting comments about words as weapons:

> One reason that many otherwise "good" people use words irresponsibly and cruelly is that they regard the injuries inflicted by words as intangible and therefore minimize the damage they can inflict....
>
> An Old Jewish teaching compares the tongue to an arrow: "Why not another weapon—a sword, for example?" one rabbi asks. "Because," he is told, "if a man unsheathes his sword to kill his friend, and his friend begs for mercy, the man may be mollified and return the sword

to its scabbard. But an arrow, once it is shot, cannot be returned."

The rabbi's comparison is more than just a useful metaphor. Because words can be used to inflict devastating and irrevocable suffering, Jewish teachings go so far as to compare cruel words to murder. A penitent thief can return the money he has stolen; a murderer, no matter how sincerely he repents, cannot restore his victim to life. Similarly, one who damages another's reputation through malicious gossip or who humiliates another publicly can never fully undo the damage....[2]

Again in this next verse, we see that our words can be as swords:

> **7 Behold, they belch forth with their mouth;**
> **Swords are in their lips...**
> **—Psalm 59**

Have you ever had someone say something to you that cut you to the quick? I suspect all of us have. I have experienced times when it felt as though a dagger had been stabbed into my heart from something someone had said. I have heard others use the same analogy. Words can wound and wound deeply.

Indirect, passive-aggressive verbal jabs, barbed comments or insults muttered under the breath can come across as demeaning. Often what is behind them is hurt of some kind or anger turned outward. The cutting remark is a childish and ineffective attempt to somehow "even the score" by verbal fencing—"You hurt me, so I'll hurt you back!"

In yet another Psalm, David refers to the words of his enemies as a deadly poison.

> **3 They sharpen their tongues as a serpent;**
> **Poison of a viper is under their lips.**
>
> **—Psalm 140**

These references suggest that David must have experienced his share of hurtful words! We obviously have no control over how others speak, but we can choose how *we* will use our words. We can be careful not to wield them as a vicious weapon that causes needless injury to others.

GOSSIP AND SLANDER

There are a multitude of Scriptural admonitions against gossip and slander. Pastor Lee Korner offers these simple working definitions of both words to help us discern when we may be participating in these exceedingly unhealthy activities:

> *"Gossip is listening to and then repeating something you didn't believe when you heard it."*

> *"Slander is murdering someone's moral character in front of witnesses."*

Webster's definition of gossip is:

> "Rumor or report of an intimate or sensational nature."

Although there are countless ways in which our words can be damaging and destructive, slander merits a special note here. *Webster's* defines it this way:

> "The utterance of false charges or misrepresentations which defame and damage another's reputation."

Slander does such incredible damage—it is like raping the character of another person, without him being present to defend himself. It is to our shame that all too often individuals within the body of Christ at large are guilty of slanderous speech. Unfortunately, many times we are as bad (or worse) about gossip and slander as unbelievers, which certainly does not honor the Lord.

Rabbi Telushkin makes these observations about gossip and slander:

> Gossip often is so interesting that it impels many of us to violate the Golden Rule to "Do unto others as you would have others do unto you." Although we are likely to acknowledge that we would want embarrassing information about ourselves kept quiet, many of us refuse to be equally discreet concerning others' sensitive secrets....
>
> The most grievous violation of ethical speech is, of course, the spreading of malicious falsehoods, what Jewish law calls *"motzi shem ra,"* or "giving another a bad name" [slander]. To destroy someone's good name is to commit a kind of murder—that is why it is called "character assassination." Indeed, it has led to literal murder. During Europe's devastating fourteenth-century Black Plague, anti-Semites and others seeking scapegoats spread the lie that Jews had caused the Plague by poisoning village wells. Within a few months, enraged mobs murdered tens of thousands of Jews....
>
> A Jewish folktale, set in nineteenth-century Eastern Europe, tells of a man who went through a small community slandering the rabbi. One day, feeling suddenly remorseful, he begged the rabbi for forgiveness and offered to undergo any form of penance to make amends. The rabbi told him to take a feather pillow from his home, cut it open, scatter the feathers to the wind. The man did as he was told and returned to the rabbi. He asked, "Am I now forgiven?"

"Almost," came the response. "You just have to perform one last task: Go and gather all the feathers."

"But that's impossible," the man protested, "for the wind has already scattered them."

"Precisely," the rabbi answered.[3]

This story illustrates well the far-reaching damage that can be done to someone's reputation by passing on negative comments.

If we hear something disparaging about someone, it is not uncommon to then harbor a question or a doubt about that individual. In fact, it is difficult to do otherwise. His character has been maligned in our eyes. Instead, we should first avoid listening to gossip and slander, and encourage the person who wishes to share such garbage with us to go directly to the person in question with his complaints, whatever they may be. If we do hear something that defames the character of another in our eyes, Jesus instructs us as to what to do, in Matthew 18:15-17. We should go to that individual directly to try to clear it up. Following this Scriptural pattern for dealing with difficulties in the church is *powerful spiritual warfare*, though seldom recognized as such and rarely practiced. It doesn't allow evil to get a foothold in our midst and it provides an opportunity for problems to be addressed in the way that is most effective—*at the root.*

A friend shared this story with me of a strategy for confronting gossip that worked for her niece:

One of my nieces, Rachel, age 12, was being gossiped about endlessly. The little girl doing all the damage was dreadfully jealous of Rachel's looks and sweet disposition, but Rachel was very hurt as, one by one, her friends turned away from her. She asked me for advice since ignoring the situation wasn't helping.

I reasoned thus: evil thrives on secrecy and darkness. How can light be introduced? So I told her that no matter where they were, the next time this girl started whispering to someone else about her, Rachel should repeat everything being spoken, loudly enough for all the girls and parents to hear. For example, "Hey everybody, so and so says, 'Rachel is sleeping around.'" She should repeat it word for word, just like an echo or mimic. I told Rachel not to deny anything said about her but just to repeat it. If she denied what was said, it would be Lady Macbeth all over again. But if she brought it out into the open, her innocence would become apparent, since she wouldn't deliberately malign her own character.

It worked like a charm! Rachel felt like she was back in control and the gossiping young lady was shamed into silence. (Shocked, too, I might add. Rachel previously had confronted her and asked her why she was spreading lies, only to have her deny everything.)[4]

Often gossip and slander are referenced in the same breath, such as in the following Proverb. Solomon warns us not to associate with a gossip:

> **19 He who goes about as a slanderer reveals secrets,
> Therefore do not associate with a gossip.**
> **—Proverbs 20**

Jesus Himself warned His followers to take care what they listened to. In my mind, this includes listening to gossip and slander. Don't do it!

> **24 And He was saying to them, "Take care what you listen to. By your standard of measure it shall be measured to you; and more shall be given you besides."**
> **—Mark 4**

We read earlier that the Lord hates a false witness who utters lies and one who spreads strife among brothers (Prov. 6:16-19). False witness and the spreading of strife among the brethren *must cease* if the church is ever to be the *light* and *salt* that God wants us to be. If our words and our actions are loving, then the message is loud and clear. *If we speak about love, yet practice slander, we are communicating a very muddled message at best.*

In writing to the church in Rome, Paul described people whom God gave over to a depraved mind. He listed *gossips* and *slanderers* right along with "haters of God," "inventors of evil" and the rest.

> **29 ...being filled with all unrighteousness, wicked-ness, greed, evil; full of envy, murder, strife, deceit, malice; *they are* gossips,**
> **30 slanderers, haters of God, insolent, arrogant, boastful, inventors of evil, disobedient to parents,...**
> **—Romans 1**

Likewise, in listing the deeds of the flesh to the Galatians, Paul includes *enmities, strife, outbursts of anger, disputes, dissensions* and *factions* in the same list with *idolatry, immorality* and other things that will keep us from inheriting the kingdom of God (Gal. 5:19-21). Take another look at these six things and consider what they have in common:

1. enmities
2. strife
3. outbursts of anger
4. disputes
5. dissensions
6. factions

It is noteworthy that all of these generally involve *our words* in some way. There are always reasons why people do the things they do, including speaking unedifying words. Hurt or jealousy may motivate us to want to hurt the other person, by gossip and slander, for example, or an angry verbal jab.

Sometimes Christianity is erroneously looked upon as consisting of harsh lists of do's and don'ts: "If you do this or that, you're a bad person." In applying Scriptural principles, it can be helpful to look behind our behaviors to see what is motivating us. Often it is not that we *intend* to do harm, but, as I mentioned in Chapter 1, something may have happened to us to cause pain and anger that we are needing to overcome. We have areas in our heart that need healing so that our words can change. If you are a chronic gossip, for example, trying to grit your teeth and stop gossiping, without looking at what is motivating your behavior, can be futile.

In his book, *Reality Therapy*, Dr. William Glasser states that we all have four basic needs: to love; to be loved; to feel worthwhile; to be accepted.[5] We all also have within us the propensity to do the kinds of things listed on the previous page in a twisted effort to get our needs met in ineffective and unhealthy ways. Fear and selfishness can be the impetus. However, if we seek to get needs met in these ways that are hurtful to others, it will backfire. The key to wholesome living is to get our needs met without hurting someone else. That is where God's ways—which are far above our ways—are always much better in the long run (Is. 55:8-9).

Ultimately, it is the character and love of the Lord within us that will make lasting changes in our behavior, including our speech. Apprehending how much He truly loves us and wants the best for us frees us from feeling like we have to perform or earn love and liberates us to do what is right.

Author Luke Rader makes these observations about the damage done by the careless use of our tongues in circulating falsehood:

> None of us for the moment would think of taking a dagger and going among our brethren, slashing, cutting, and stabbing whoever of them crossed our path, yet the harm so inflicted upon them would not be nearly as damaging as that which our tongues constantly inflict upon each other....There is too much at stake in the careless use of our tongues....
>
> In one church, some years ago, over three hundred people withdrew their fellowship because of a falsehood circulated by one woman. Only God can estimate the damage done, first to His work in the church and second to those who withdrew....True, they should have investigated the story before believing it, but when reputable people repeat a tale, even a lie takes on the respectable clothing of truth. For, the more favor and honor God showers upon us, the more weight our words bear....
>
> We need to be especially on guard against evil speaking when we are going through a hard testing, a time of chastening, for then it is easy for discouragement, resentment, and bitterness to get into our souls for in such times of heaviness, everything seems dark, faith is hard to grasp, and our bitterness may flare out to defile many. By such careless unbridling of our tongues in backbiting, we leave our proper place of trust and fellowship with God as priests in the Holy Place.
>
> Evil speaking and criticism are sure evidences of conceit and pride in our hearts. They spring from an assumption of superiority and mastery which exalts us to the position of judging others. As James puts it, "Speak not evil one of another, brethren, He that speaketh evil of

his brother, and judgeth his brother, speaketh evil of the law, and judgeth the law; but if thou judge the law, thou art not a doer of the law, but a judge" (James 4:11).[6]

Isaiah speaks further about slander, saying that a rogue devises wicked schemes to destroy others with slander. In contrast, he says that a noble man makes and executes noble plans with integrity (Is. 32:7-8).

Satan is referred to as the "accuser of the brethren," who accuses Christians before God day and night (Rev. 12:10). When we accuse our brothers before others (slander), we are playing on Satan's team, which is not very bright if we want to have a winning team! Winning teams are those who learn to work together in mutual support, in spite of differences. Certainly accusing our brothers and sisters in Christ does nothing to glorify God or help expand His kingdom. *We can each resolve right now to strive never to be guilty of accusing one of our brethren before another and, thus, operating as an ally to our enemy in the spiritual war.*

DISPUTES, DECEIT AND OTHER DAMAGING WORDS

In writing to Timothy, Paul warned that constant friction and all manner of other ungodly things arise out of disputes about words:

3 If anyone advocates a different doctrine, and does not agree with sound words, those of our Lord Jesus Christ, and with the doctrine conforming to godliness,

4 he is conceited *and* understands nothing; but he has a morbid interest in controversial questions and

disputes about words, out of which arise envy, strife, abusive language, evil suspicions,

5 and constant friction between men of depraved mind and deprived of the truth, who suppose that godliness is a means of gain.

—1 Timothy 6

More simply put, envy, strife, abusive language, evil suspicions and constant friction are all things that can arise out of disputes about words. It is interesting to consider that one becomes *depraved* when *deprived* of the truth. Once again, it becomes apparent that we each need to learn to guard our tongues wisely.

In the same letter, Paul instructs his protégé to avoid worldly and empty chatter:

20 O Timothy, guard what has been entrusted to you, avoiding worldly *and* empty chatter *and* the opposing arguments of what is falsely called "knowledge"—

21 which some have professed and thus gone astray from the faith.

—1 Timothy 6

Think of a time when you had an argument or discussion that was pointless and obviously going no-where. I have had more of those than I care to admit. In fact, I recall Jack and I facing this problem, especially in the first year-and-a-half of our marriage, and stopping to say, "What are we arguing about?" Pointless opposing arguments are futile and an energy drain. I must confess that sometimes I have been guilty of caring more about making my point and *being "right"* than considering the effect of my words on another person.

What is the point of a tug-of-war? If you give it some thought, I think you will agree that the only purpose is a show of strength and *to win*. This is a good visual image of the power struggle going back and forth with pointless arguments. How do you take care of this problem? Simply drop the rope. Christ teaches that real power is in surrender.

What do you think Paul means by *"opposing arguments of what is falsely called knowledge"*? I think that sometimes we get so insistent that we have "the truth" about something with our "opposing arguments" that we lose sight altogether of what knowledge is all about. *The truth doesn't have to defend itself.*

We read some references earlier wherein David said our tongue can be as a sword. Here he speaks of deceitful words being like a *sharp razor*...that is, they cut!

> 2 **Your tongue devises destruction,**
>   **Like a sharp razor, O worker of deceit.**
> 3 **You love evil more than good,**
>   **Falsehood more than speaking what is right.**
> 4 **You love all words that devour,**
>   **O deceitful tongue.**
>
> **—Psalm 52**

Words can *devour* (vs. 4)—everything from peace of mind to a person's livelihood! Loving falsehood more than speaking what is right is deceitful and ultimately damaging, even if you think you can rationalize it at the time.

An acquaintance of mine was recently recounting that she had attended a women's retreat hosted by her church. She had been appalled at the way the women were speaking negatively about their husbands. When they looked to her for comment, she said simply, "I love my husband and I think he's just wonderful." This was in sharp contrast to the degrading remarks made by some of the other women regarding their mates. It is always easy to look for the negative and to be critical, but that does not edify us nor anyone listening, and certainly not the person whom we are criticizing.

It is my personal belief that publicly speaking disparagingly about one's spouse is one of the most belittling things a mate can do. Besides dishonoring the spouse, it does not speak well of the one doing the criticizing. (It is my belief that if you have a bone to pick with your spouse, it can and should be discussed in private, not in front of others where it only serves to humiliate and produce resentments.) We are to honor one another, and I believe this includes honoring one another in our speech.

Solomon put it this way:

> **32 The lips of the righteous bring forth what is**
> **acceptable,**
> **But the mouth of the wicked, what is perverted.**
> **—Proverbs 10**

I want to be one of the righteous whose lips bring forth what is acceptable, not what is perverted.

In the book of Isaiah, the Lord said He would be there when the people called, if certain conditions were met. The first one listed is that they remove from their midst the wicked yoke of *speaking accusation*:

> **9 "Then you will call, and the Lord will answer;**
> **You will cry, and He will say, 'Here I am.'**
> **If you remove the yoke from your midst,**
> **The pointing of the fingers, and speaking**
> **wickedness,..."**
> **—Isaiah 58**

Words of accusation and wickedness can be very damaging, and the damage done by ill-spoken words can be hard to repair. The use of the word "yoke" gives me the feeling that God looks at this as a form of bondage from which we need to be freed. Perhaps the bondage is that anything we practice can become *habitual,* and bad habits are hard to break.

Chances are that all of us have, at some point, said something to someone or made an accusation and later wished we could take back those words. It's as though the words have a power of their own that can come back and haunt us. Better to avoid damaging speech in the first place.

Unfortunately, small factions within churches have often been guilty of backbiting, finger pointing (blame) and accusation against other members in their own body! Perhaps you have run into this. It has caused splinter-groups and disruption in many churches, even resulting in nasty church splits, which are never without casualties. Finding a better way to work through our differences may be difficult, but the energy to do so will be well worth it.

GRUMBLING AND COMPLAINING

Jack and I have a black and white cat named Feliz. In every way she is a lovely animal, except one. Sometimes she will start meowing for no apparent reason and she won't stop! I am not talking about crying to get in or out, or because she is hungry or thirsty. Since we don't speak fluent "cat," it is difficult to understand what she wants at these times. It doesn't seem to be anything in particular. She is just complaining, because things are not going her way. When this occurs in the middle of the night or some other inconvenient time, it becomes extremely annoying. At times like that, it really seems as though she just likes to complain indiscriminately.

I don't think anybody likes a complainer. My mother used to say, "Quit your bellyaching, grousing and complaining." At one point in my childhood, she came up with what I thought even then was an ingenious idea—a "grudge jar." We were to write down all of our complaints and put them in there. She worked full time as a nursing supervisor and I can understand how she got sick and tired of three children repeatedly expressing their beefs, as most parents likely do.

Peter admonishes us to be hospitable to one another *without complaint* (1 Pet. 4:9). Paul instructs us to, *"do all things without grumbling or disputing so that we may prove ourselves blameless, innocent and above reproach"* (Phil. 2:14-15). He tells the church in Corinth that the accounts about what happened to the Israelites in the wilderness were written for our instruction. Some of them grumbled and complained and were destroyed (1 Cor. 10:9-11).

Personally, I think that the practice of grumbling and complaining brings its own kind of destruction. It breeds an atmosphere of discontent which is certain to have ill effects. Once again, we reap what we sow. Grumbling and murmuring serve no constructive mission. No wonder the Lord despises these things so!

During a recent local radio broadcast, Pastor Jon Courson challenged the listeners to *fast from complaining for twenty-four hours*. I think this is a great idea and one I plan to implement in my own life. (I already know that purposefully putting aside complaining helps a marriage!) Several days after this broadcast, a friend commented to me that she did not realize how much complaining she really did on a regular basis, until she tried this idea. It was eye-opening to her![7]

HAVE YOU EVER CONSIDERED THAT PEOPLE ARE MORE IMPORTANT THAN YOUR PROCLAMATION OF "TRUTH"?

Jesus said that *"the truth will set you free,"* and indeed it will (John 8:32). However, He also only said and did what He saw the Father doing (John 5:19). I don't believe He ran around beating people over the head with things He knew to be true. There is a time to speak truth and a time to remain silent (Ecc. 3:1, 7). By the very nature of truth, sometimes it takes time to be understood.

I submit that people—that is, their feelings and sensibilities—are more important than your right or mine to declare something we perceive as truth in a way that will demolish the individual we are addressing. (Some may refer to that as being "brutally frank.") Truth edifies; it makes the path clear. Its goal or aim is to make you better. It is not a club to try to convince someone else that you are right and he or she is wrong. Generally speaking, trying to use it that way will only serve to invoke defensiveness in your listener.

When truth is spoken in love, there is a sensitivity to timing and delivery. The message may not always feel good or be what we would like to hear. Some truth is indeed hard to bear. When it is truth about our behavior, it may bring conviction to change, but it should not condemn. That is not the way of Christ.

CRITICISM, FAULT-FINDING, DISPARAGING REMARKS

I single out criticism and fault-finding, as it can be easy to fall into this kind of mentality, without even realizing we are coming across as critical and judgmental. Yet these things can be very destructive to relationships. Tuning into how we are being unnecessarily critical can help our relationships.

In a frequently-cited study of marital conflict, Dr. John Gottman came to this fascinating discovery:

> What really separates contented couples from those in marital misery is a healthy balance between their positive and negative feelings and actions toward each other. In our research, we found that in stable marriages there was a very specific ratio that exists between the number of a couple's positive interactions—touching, smiling, paying compliments, laughing—and their negative ones. The magic ratio is five to one. In other words, as long as there is five times as much positive feeling and interaction between husband and wife as there is negative, we found that the marriage was likely to be stable. Based solely on this ratio, we were able to predict whether couples were likely to divorce.[8]

Although this study is speaking about all kinds of interactions—not just verbal—verbal interactions certainly play into this interesting predictive ratio. You might want to consider the close relationships in your life, whether with a spouse, a child, a sibling, or someone else. What percentage of your remarks are positive and uplifting, as compared to ones that could be interpreted as negative, critical, fault-finding or demeaning?

Of course, there are legitimate times to express concerns, opinions, and constructive criticism. The key operative word here is *constructive*. However, in actuality, much of what we may rationalize as being "constructive," purely and simply, is fault-finding. It serves no healthy or edifying purpose.

B.F. Skinner is a renowned psychologist from Harvard University. His research makes it abundantly clear that a child—or anyone else—learns significantly more from being praised for what they do right than from being punished for what they do wrong.[9]

In highlighting in this chapter some of the specific ways our words can be used negatively, I am well aware that I personally have a long ways to go. I can do a lot of growing regarding a more edifying use of my speech. We are all in this one together, and as with any area of growth, there is a *process* to learning how to use our words more constructively. Part of that process entails initially becoming aware of how our words can be hurtful.

THE GIFT OF CARING
EXPRESSED VOCALLY

In the following excerpt from *A Touch of Wonder*, Arthur Gordon graphically illustrates the power of verbally expressed emotions, criticism and encouragement to affect destiny:

> It has been said that you tend to become what you think you are. But what you think you are is colored, inevitably, by what you conceive other people's opinion of you to be. If you think they are critical (or even indifferent), your self-esteem shrinks, and with it your capacity for living.

Some criticism, no doubt, is constructive, but too much is a subtle poison. A friend of mine told me of a club he belonged to in his undergraduate days at the University of Wisconsin. The members were a group of brilliant boys, some with real literary talent. At each meeting one of them would read a story or essay he had written and submit it to the criticism of the others. No punches were pulled; each manuscript was mercilessly dissected. The sessions were so brutal that the club members dubbed themselves *The Stranglers*. This club was strictly a masculine affair, so naturally the coeds formed a comparable group of their own known as *The Wranglers*. They, too, read their manuscripts aloud. But the criticism was much gentler. In fact, there was almost none at all. The Wranglers hunted for kind things to say. All efforts, however feeble, were encouraged.

The payoff came about twenty years later, when some alumnus made an analysis of his classmates' careers. Of all the bright young talent in The Stranglers, not one had made a literary reputation of any kind. Out of The Wranglers had come half a dozen successful writers, some of national prominence, led by Marjorie Kinnan Rawlings, who wrote *The Yearling*. Coincidence? Hardly. The amount of basic talent in the two groups was much the same. But The Wranglers gave one another a lift. The Stranglers promoted self-criticism, self-disparagement, self-doubt. In choosing a name for themselves, they had been wiser than they knew.

Awareness of the power of affection to unlock human capabilities is at least two thousand years old ("A new commandment I give unto you, That ye love one another..."). But affection is not much good unless it is expressed. What's more, I have a notion that unexpressed feelings have a tendency to shrink, wither, and ultimately die. Putting an emotion into words gives it a life and a reality that otherwise it doesn't have.[10]

THE IMPACT OF OUR WORDS

Again, I would like to cite an example from a story Paul Hegstrom shared on one of his audio tapes.[11] He was discussing the subject of *imprinting*, which can happen even with babies just weeks old, long before they intellectually understand language and the meaning of words. It has been shown that messages can be imprinted into their hearts and emotional lives even at that very young age. (Actually, it has been proven that babies even in the womb can be imprinted. They recognize and respond to music their mothers repeatedly listen to while pregnant.)

When Paul and Judy's eldest daughter, Tammy, was just a couple of weeks old, she woke up crying loudly one night, as babies do when they are hungry. Judy handed the baby to Paul to lay on his chest and said, "You hold her while I go get the bottle." He did so and the newborn child proceeded to scream and holler at the top of her lungs. After a few moments of this, he held the baby up and screamed in full voice, "I hate babies!"

Years later when Tammy was grown, married and had a child of her own, it was a puzzle as to why she would always come between Paul and his young grandson. Anytime Paul went to pick up the child or try to show him some affection, Tammy was right there interceding. On one special holiday occasion, a family gathering, Paul reached for the boy and Tammy snatched him up and took him into another room. This time Paul confronted the no-longer-deniable issue and said, "Tammy, what is wrong? Why is it that you do this?" She turned and literally screamed at him, "Because Daddy hates babies!" Broken, he asked her, "Tammy, where did that come from?" She had no idea. Of course, he and Judy knew all too well. It was from that day when she, as a baby of just a couple of weeks old, had that message imprinted into her subconscious by her father, in a moment of sleepless frustration and anger.

Do not take lightly the words that you speak. Watch carefully what you say in times of emotional upset, as your words can leave a lasting mark on the life of another and sometimes can create wreckage that subsequently can be very difficult to restore.

You are a *mighty mouth.*

chapter 3

USING OUR WORDS
FOR GOOD

The exciting and positive news is that, just as our words have power to devastate and destroy, words can be utilized instead to bring life, hope, joy and edification. Proverbs goes so far as to say that wise words are a *"fountain of life"*!

> 14 The teaching of the wise is a fountain of life,
>   To turn aside from the snares of death.
> —Proverbs 13

THE POWER OF WORDS
TO INSTRUCT AND EDIFY

A person who is articulate wields tremendous power with his words, whether or not he is aware of it. One individual in particular comes to mind whom I know does not consider herself to be a strong person. But when she speaks, it is with such eloquence and sometimes forcefulness that she has no small effect on others around her. She is, without a doubt, a person of influence, much more than she realizes.

Language can be a tool to motivate people, to organize, to instruct, to encourage and to inspire. Solomon accurately observes that a ready and appropriate answer brings joy and a good word spoken in timely fashion is a delight:

> **23 A man has joy in an apt answer,
>   And how delightful is a timely word!**
> **—Proverbs 15**

Undoubtedly, we all have experienced situations wherein a word of encouragement was spoken to us just when we really needed it. Perhaps it was the very thing that bolstered our spirits and gave us the courage to press on, even in the face of difficult circumstances. Your words of encouragement judiciously shared with others can, likewise, be a lifeline in a time of need.

As an example of what I mean by this, I would like to quote the following story:

One day, when I was a freshman in high school, I saw a kid from my class walking home from school. His name was Kyle. It looked like he was carrying all of his books. I thought to myself, "Why would anyone bring home all his books on a Friday? He must really be a nerd."

I had quite a weekend planned (parties and a football game with my friends the next afternoon), so I shrugged my shoulders and went on. As I was walking, I saw a bunch of kids running toward him. They ran at him, knocking all his books out of his arms and tripping him so he landed in the dirt. His glasses went flying, and I saw them land in the grass about ten feet from him.

He looked up and I saw this terrible sadness in his eyes. My heart went out to him. So, I jogged over to him, as he crawled around looking for his glasses, and I saw a tear in his eye. As I handed him his glasses, I said,

"Those guys are jerks. They really should get lives." He looked at me and said, "Hey, thanks!" There was a big smile on his face. It was one of those smiles that showed real gratitude.

I helped him pick up his books, and asked him where he lived. As it turned out, he lived near me, so I asked him why I had never seen him before. He said he had gone to private school before now. I would have never hung out with a private school kid before. We talked all the way home, and I carried his books.

He turned out to be a pretty cool kid. I asked him if he wanted to play football on Saturday with me and my friends. He said yes. We hung all weekend and the more I got to know Kyle, the more I liked him. And my friends thought the same of him.

Monday morning came, and there was Kyle with the huge stack of books again. I stopped him and said, "Boy, you are gonna really build some serious muscles with this pile of books everyday!" He just laughed and handed me half the books.

Over the next four years, Kyle and I became best friends. When we were seniors, we began to think about college. Kyle decided on Georgetown, and I was going to Duke. I knew that we would always be friends, that the miles would never be a problem. He was going to be a doctor, and I was going for business on a football scholarship. Kyle was valedictorian of our class. I teased him all the time about being a nerd. He had to prepare a speech for graduation. I was so glad it wasn't me having to get up there and speak.

Graduation day, I saw Kyle. He looked great. He was one of those guys who really found himself during high school. He filled out and actually looked good in glasses. He had more dates than me and all the girls loved him! Boy, sometimes I was jealous. Today was one of those days. I could see that he was nervous about his speech.

So, I smacked him on the back and said, "Hey, big guy, you'll be great!" He looked at me with one of those looks (the really grateful one) and smiled. "Thanks," he said.

As he started his speech, he cleared his throat, and began. "Graduation is a time to thank those who helped you make it through those tough years. Your parents, your teachers, your siblings, maybe a coach...but mostly your friends. I am here to tell all of you that being a friend to someone is the best gift you can give them. I am going to tell you a story." I just looked at my friend with disbelief as he told the story of the first day we met. He had planned to kill himself over the weekend. He talked of how he had cleaned out his locker so his mom wouldn't have to do it later and was carrying his stuff home. He looked hard at me and gave me little smile. "Thankfully, I was saved. My friend saved me from doing the unspeakable."

I heard the gasp go through the crowd as this handsome, popular boy told us all about his weakest moment. I saw his Mom and Dad looking at me and smiling that same grateful smile. Not until that moment did I realize its depth.

Never underestimate the power of your actions. With one small gesture, you can change a person's life. For better or for worse. God puts us all in each other's lives to impact one another in some way. Look for God in others. Each day is a gift from God! Don't forget to say, "Thank you!"[1]

This was a case wherein kind words, backed up by action, literally had a life-saving effect. We are not always privileged to see the fruit of our positive words in the lives of others, but every once in a while we may get a glimpse, as this thoughtful student did on his graduation day.

A woman who reviewed this manuscript also shared a fresh example of how a word of encouragement came to her in a recent moment of need:

> While I was sitting in the waiting room proofing this page, God sent a woman to witness to me and lift me up. I've been concerned about my daughter's upcoming surgery and although she knew nothing about that, she sang to me a verse from Joshua—"Be ye strong and of good courage and do not be dismayed."[2]

MORE ON GOOD WORDS FROM PROVERBS

As I mentioned earlier, the book of Proverbs has much to say about our words, both good and bad. Here are a few more insights about the power of our words to *instruct* and to *do good*. I like to actually print out many of the Scriptures for you, so you can see for yourself what the Bible has to say on this critical subject:

1 **A gentle answer turns away wrath,
But a harsh word stirs up anger.**
2 **The tongue of the wise makes knowledge acceptable,
But the mouth of fools spouts folly....**
7 **The lips of the wise spread knowledge,
But the hearts of fools are not so.**
—Proverbs 15

It is significant to realize that with our words we can either stir up anger or subdue it. The choice is ours.

Jack and I were eating at one of our favorite local restaurants recently. I explained to the waitress what I wanted and she acted like she wasn't sure they could fulfill my request. I replied—I guess not very sensi-tively—that of course they could, for I had had the dish there that way many times before.

After the waitress had left our table, Jack made the observation that I had offended her. Her subsequent syrupy and overly-patronizing response was an interesting defense mechanism to my unnecessarily exasperated-sounding words. As one who hates to ever offend a fly, I regretted my overreaction in the way I had spoken to her. Jack was right.

It was a small thing, and in no way a major blow up. I am generally a pretty perceptive person, relatively tuned into people's emotional reactions, but this one was subtle enough that I would have missed it, had Jack not made a comment about it. I did not need to take out my irritation on the waitress with the *tone* of my words. Even in small ways, what we speak affects those around us, as this instance so clearly demonstrated.

Solomon is considered to be the wisest man who ever lived. This next passage reveals that he determined to speak noble things and what was righteous and straight-forward. In so doing, he had confidence that his words would produce right things (vs. 6) and his instruction would be more valuable than gold or jewels:

> 6 **"Listen, for I shall speak noble things;**
> **And the opening of my lips will produce right**
> **things.**
> 7 **"For my mouth will utter truth;**
> **And wickedness is an abomination to my lips.**
> 8 **"All the utterances of my mouth are in righ-**
> **teousness;**
> **There is nothing crooked or perverted in them.**

9 "They are all straightforward to him who understands,
And right to those who find knowledge.
10 "Take my instruction, and not silver,
And knowledge rather than choicest gold.
11 "For wisdom is better than jewels;
And all desirable things can not compare with
her...."

—Proverbs 8

I am inspired by Solomon's strong stance and decla-
ration that his mouth would utter truth. I want to be able
to say the same.

Another beautiful verse in Proverbs that I especially
love says this:

24 Pleasant words are a honeycomb,
Sweet to the soul and healing to the bones.

—Proverbs 16

Besides a sweet taste, another characteristic of honey
is that it is sticky. Just as you can return and lick the
sweet honeycomb repeatedly, so do you return to sweet
words for nourishment of your soul. Even after all the
honey is gone, there is still a sweet aroma that lingers.

It is encouraging to know that our words themselves
can minister life and healing to others! Once again, this
verse attests to the fact that something we choose to say
may bring joy to another or be the very word of encouragement, hope or inspiration that helps him (or her) to
make it through a tough situation.

Most of us have witnessed a loud, belligerent,
argumentative person obnoxiously making a point.
Generally, the typical reaction to that type of approach is
to build a wall of resistance, rather than being persuaded

to change one's position. Solomon shared this insight about more effective communication:

> **21 The wise in heart will be called discerning,**
> **And sweetness of speech increases persuasiveness...**
>
> **23 The heart of the wise teaches his mouth,**
> **And adds persuasiveness to his lips.**
> **—Proverbs 16**

Did you notice that sweet, pleasantly-spoken words can increase our persuasiveness? In contrast to a pushy, forceful individual, if one is approached graciously by someone who kindly presents his case, this generally begets a greater receptivity from the listener. Harsh words cause most of us to automatically respond with defensiveness, because we feel we have been attacked. (Attacks require defense or surrender.) A person who is busy being defensive rarely is able to fully hear the heart of what is being spoken to him.

This brings to mind a parable I heard as a child about the sun and the wind. A man is out walking with a warm coat on and the sun and wind are having a discussion about who can make him take off his coat. The wind, of course, is certain that it will be the winner. So it blows and blows and blows as hard as it can, attempting, from every angle possible, to blow off the man's coat. But the fierceness of the wind and gale only causes the man to wrap his coat all the more tightly about himself, in an effort to protect himself from the wintery blast.

Then the sun says, "Let me try!" So it shines, and it shines, and it shines, brightly and warmly. Very soon the man is unbuttoning his coat. Before much longer, he takes it off and carries it. The warmth of the sun is easily much more persuasive than all of the blasting, blowing and commotion that the wind can muster. So it is with pleasant words. A wise man *"teaches his mouth"* (vs. 23), and in so doing increases the persuasiveness of his lips.

JESUS SPOKE GRACIOUS WORDS

Luke lets us know that Jesus spoke *"gracious words"* that caused people to wonder:

> **22 And all were speaking well of Him, and wondering at the gracious words which were falling from His lips; and they were saying, "Is this not Joseph's son?"**
> **—Luke 4**

If you read the preceding verse in context, you will see that Jesus had stood up in the synagogue to read from the prophet Isaiah. He stopped reading, closed the scroll and sat down, right in the middle of a sentence! He was reading from Isaiah 61, and He ended on the gracious word—that is, the release of captives, recovery of sight to the blind, the setting free of the downtrodden and proclaiming the favorable year of the Lord. The sentence in Isaiah continues with, *"...and the day of vengeance of our God...."* He stopped reading on *grace*, knowing that the day of vengeance was for a different time.

As well as being our Saviour, Jesus is also our Example of how to live a victorious Christian life.[3] We can learn much from the words that He spoke, the *way* that He spoke, and the effect that His words had on others, as revealed in Scripture.

OUR WORDS REFLECT OUR HEART

Jesus lets us know that we will give account for our words in the day of judgment and He indicates that our words flow out of that which fills our heart. Therefore, it behooves us to examine our speech carefully to see if it is glorifying to God. He said:

33 "Either make the tree good, and its fruit good; or make the tree rotten, and its fruit rotten; for the tree is known by its fruit.

34 "You brood of vipers, how can you, being evil, speak what is good? For the mouth speaks out of that which fills the heart.

35 "The good man out of *his* good treasure brings forth what is good; and the evil man out of *his* evil treasure brings forth what is evil.

36 "And I say to you, that every careless word that men shall speak, they shall render account for it in the day of judgment.

37 "For by your words you shall be justified, and by your words you shall be condemned."

—Matthew 12

The *New King James Version* poetically states the latter half of verse 34 this way:

"For out of the abundance of the heart the mouth speaks."

Also descriptive is the *New International Version:*

"For out of the overflow of the heart the mouth speaks."

However you want to state it, it becomes clear that our words will reflect what is in our heart.

There is no doubt that our actions carry great weight. James says that faith without works is dead (James 2:17). But in the preceding passage we see that God attaches an equal responsibility to what comes out of our mouth. I don't believe that the importance of *both* what we do and what we say can be overstated. None of us just naturally have thorough mastery over our behavior and our mouth. Yet in essence Jesus is saying, "Look, this is really important! You are going to be held accountable!" Thank God we have a Savior!

If you ever wonder what's going on with yourself, just pay attention to what is coming out of your mouth. It can be highly enlightening as to the state of your inner man.

When Jack and I were first dating, he shared an impactive story with me that was helpful in something I was facing at the time. A young Indian was speaking with his grandfather about some inner turmoil that he was experiencing. The conflict was a struggle about what he should do. He described that it felt like a war raging in his heart, a struggle of good and bad. Searching for a way to explain, he described it like two dogs fighting, a black dog and a white dog. His wise old grandfather patiently listened. At his grandson's conclusion, he reassured him that everything would work out. The dubious lad queried, "How can you be so sure? I don't share your confidence." His grandfather smiled knowingly and advised him, "Because you will feed the white dog."

Knowing what to do does not automatically mean that we always do it. But if our *goal* is to speak good, edifying words, and those are the kinds of thoughts we feed and nurture, we will grow and improve in our execution of what we know to be right and desirable behavior.

The first three steps in any 12-step Recovery Program offer a sound foundation for our spiritual journey. Very simply stated, they are: "I can't. He can. I think I'll let Him." Coming to a place of realization that we need God's power to transform us, that we can't do it on our own, and utter surrender and yieldedness to that reality is a strong starting point for healthy change.

So we learned from Jesus' words in Matthew 12 that what we say is related to what fills our heart. If we stop to consider where our words originate, it becomes obvious that our words come from our *thoughts*. We think it before we say it.

Taking this another step back, Jesus' comment about this makes sense, since it is really *our heart* (our center of feelings) that determines our thoughts and, consequently, our words. Inevitably, we are going to speak out of that which is deep within us. *Webster's Dictionary* gives these meanings for *heart*, as I believe it is used in Matthew 12:34, quoted earlier:

> "The whole personality including intellectual as well as emotional functions or traits; the central or innermost part."

Jesus also teaches specifically that evil thoughts come out of the heart:

> **18 "But the things that proceed out of the mouth come from the heart, and those defile the man.**
> **19 "For out of the heart come evil thoughts, murders, adulteries, fornications, thefts, false witness, slanders."**
>
> **—Matthew 15**

Our thoughts come from the basic intent of our heart, whether it be good or bad. If we set our heart on Jesus and positive things, it will have a direct effect on our thought life and, subsequently, on our words. Actively taking command over the realm of our thought life will bear good fruit in our words. For some constructive help in doing this, I would recommend committing these verses to memory: 2 Corinthians 10:5, Philippians 4:8, Isaiah 26:3, Romans 8:5-6. These and a number of others are typed out in the Appendix, for your convenience.

Paul instructed the church at Phillipi to focus their minds on *good things*, in one of my all-time personal favorite verses in Scripture:

> **8 Finally, brethren, whatever is true, whatever is honorable, whatever is right, whatever is pure, whatever is lovely, whatever is of good repute, if there is any excellence and if anything worthy of praise, let your mind dwell on these things.**
>
> **—Philippians 4**

Truly putting this powerful admonition into practice on a regular basis has the potential to revolutionize our lives. There is no shortage of bad news, pain, misery, injustices and disappointments. All of these things are a part of life. The choice as to where we allow our attention to dwell is our own—on the negative circumstances or on the good that we can glean from life's challenges. Choose wisely. The focus of our gaze will determine the quality of our days...and the object of our focus *will* be reflected in our words.

WORDS AS
OFFENSIVE WEAPONS

The words of our mouth can be an offensive weapon (as opposed to a weapon of destruction). As noted earlier, by the word of His mouth, the Lord created the earth and all that is in it. We are made in His image and our words, too, have tremendous power to create, to minister, to bless, and to encourage.

Each of us can determine now to use the words of our mouth as an offensive weapon for good, for God's kingdom. We can purpose to consciously avoid negative or destructive speech that tears down, deciding instead to make our words edifying. Think of our speech as having the potential to be a beacon of light and life to hurting people around us in everyday situations.

One way that our words can serve as an offensive weapon is when we choose to praise the Lord in all things, outwardly as well as inwardly, even in the midst of a difficulty or trying circumstances. Paul instructs the church at Ephesus this way:

> **18 And do not get drunk with wine, for that is dissipation, but be filled with the Spirit,**
> **19 speaking to one another in psalms and hymns and spiritual songs, singing and making melody with your heart to the Lord;**
> **20 always giving thanks for all things in the name of our Lord Jesus Christ to God, even the Father;...**
> **—Ephesians 5**

This passage outlines certain ways we can use our words constructively; however it uses terminology to which we might not readily relate. We may need to give some thought as to just what these things mean. To reiterate, Paul admonishes us to:

1. Speak to one another in psalms and hymns and spiritual songs.
2. Sing and make melody with your heart to the Lord.
3. Always give thanks for all things in the name of our Lord.

A "psalm" is defined as:

"A sacred song or poem used in worship; esp.: one of the Biblical hymns collected in the book of Psalms."[4]

A "hymn" is:

"A song of praise to God; a song of praise or joy."[5]

Webster's defines "spiritual" as:

"Of, relating to, consisting of, or affecting the spirit; relating to sacred matters...rather than temporal."[6]

And lastly, although a "song" is commonly known as a musical composition of words and music, other meanings given include these:

"A poetical composition; a habitual or characteristic manner."[7]

In short, I believe we are to let our life reflect the song of our faith through both our words and our actions. How this is manifested in individual personalities may look different.   For someone not particularly gifted musically nor inclined in that direction, it may entail something like quoting a verse from the Psalms to someone who is discouraged (the Psalms were originally songs). For example:

> **11 Why are you in despair, O my soul?**
> **And why have you become disturbed within me?**
> **Hope in God, for I shall yet praise Him,**
> **The help of my countenance, and my God.**
> **—Psalm 42**

All of us need to have truth spoken into our lives, even truths with which we may be familiar, especially in life's troublesome moments. We need to be reminded of the source of our security and hope, and that it is not in our own abilities. The spiritual truth of God's word has power to minister life, just in the simple speaking of it. This may be one reason for Paul's exhortation to the church to build up one another in this manner.

For many years, our ministry office staff memorized a new verse of Scripture together during our devotional times. We found that being accountable to one another to speak it aloud together really helped all of us to hide the word in our hearts. At one point, we really got ambitious and memorized Psalm 91 in its entirety over a number of months. This is a tremendous Psalm for anyone facing any kind of crisis. One of our employees had a son who was in the Marines at that time. News came that he was being sent overseas into the Gulf war region. Understandably, his mother was deeply grieved at the potential loss of her son in a wartime situation. She later shared how voicing that Psalm we had learned together was the saving grace that had seen her through that time of great emotional distress and concern for the safety of her only son. *Words can speak life* and, in her case, this powerful Psalm ministered healing, comfort, encouragement and hope to her extremely troubled heart.

Although speaking to someone in a psalm, a hymn or a spiritual song may not come naturally, it can be a very edifying experience. On several occasions, after teaching the word (or even in the middle of a message!), I have felt impressed to minister Scripture via the medium of song (with melody) to various individuals. I recall one instance of this in particular that was profoundly moving. I had just spoken to a ladies' group at a special luncheon in a church in Nebraska. I was prompted to begin to sing Scriptures prophetically to individual women there. As I remained in a prayerful attitude, by the time I felt impressed to conclude, the Holy Spirit had given me a personal Scripture for each woman present! A number of the ladies—nearly all strangers to me—told me afterward how appropriate their Scripture was for what they were going through at that time.

The tape of that meeting was later mailed to our ministry Partners, and one of them commented to me—many years later—how profoundly it had affected him, even hearing the songs on tape. My point is that if we take Paul's admonition seriously to speak to one another in this manner, it can have an immense impact, above and beyond our imaginings.

The Scriptures give us examples, such as David and Solomon, who chose to make their mouths vehicles of praise. David said it well in this Psalm, another favorite of mine:

> 1 **I will bless the LORD at all times;**
> **His praise shall continually be in my mouth.**

2   **My soul shall make its boast in the LORD;**
    The humble shall hear it and rejoice.
3   **O magnify the LORD with me,**
    And let us exalt His name together.

—Psalm 34

David encourages us to exalt the name of the Lord together! We too can choose to offer up vocal thanksgiving to God. Praise invites the presence of the Lord, for God inhabits the praises of His people (Ps. 22:3).

In the story of Job, we have an example of a righteous man who chose not to blame and curse God, even though he was brought to absolute ruin without cause. Essentially he lost everything (Job 1:14-22). In the midst of this great trauma, Job *chose* to *worship* God. When even his own wife encouraged him to curse God, his reply was:

10   **"...Shall we indeed accept good from God and not accept adversity?" In all this Job did not sin with his lips.**

—Job 2

In spite of all of the devastating circumstances that occurred in Job's life, we read that he did not *sin with his lips*. What an awesome example we have of trust in God's sovereignty.

The Scriptures contain plenty of examples such as this of victories over bleak-looking circumstances, when God's people *chose* to praise Him. 2 Chronicles 20:1-30 relates an exciting story of how the Lord did the fighting for Judah in the face of a great multitude of enemies that confronted them. Incidentally, "Judah" literally means *praise*. When the children of Israel first packed up their tents and left mount Sinai, the tribe of Judah was sent out first. In this passage in Chronicles, armies had come to make war against Jehoshaphat. He proclaimed a fast throughout all Judah and together they sought the Lord. Then those appointed to praise the Lord went out *in front of the army* (vs. 21-22). When they began *singing and praising,* the Lord set ambushes against their enemy and brought deliverance!

When Paul and Silas were *praying* and *singing praise* to God in prison, it was *then* that God performed a miracle to shake the prison and supernaturally free them (Acts 16:25, 26). Jesus *gave thanks* for the fish and loaves and *then* the miracle occurred of the multiplication of food and the feeding of 4,000 (Matt. 15:36-38). Peter walked on water as long as he had his eyes fixed on Jesus. The moment he shifted his focus to the wind and his troublesome circumstances, he became afraid and began to sink (Matt. 14:29-30).

Choosing to trust God and *to voice that trust by praising Him,* no matter what, releases something in the heavenly realm. Spiritual laws are activated. Satan wins a victory if he can get us to take our eyes off Jesus and put them on the discouraging circumstances. But he doesn't know what to do with a Christian who chooses to praise God in all things. Praise thwarts the schemes of the enemy against us and drives him away to pick on an easier target.

One personal way I like to praise God is by singing Christian songs. This particular tool unlocks healing for me and is a source of freedom and refreshment from stress. On the other hand, my husband would just as soon listen to Beethoven's "Ninth." What constitutes praise for each of us may differ, but the point is to let what comes out of our mouth be filled with gratitude and thanksgiving. *Praise has a way of refocusing our attention on God's goodness and capability to meet our every need.* We don't give Him praise because God *needs* anything from us. Praise is for *our* good, as well as being a step of obedience.

Our words—spoken in the power of Jesus' name and the anointing of the Holy Spirit—also can be used in a very practical way in deliverance and healing. Jesus is the One who heals and brings deliverance, but we can be used by God as instruments of healing, vessels through which spiritual gifts flow. *The use of our words to minister healing or deliverance is an offensive weapon in our spiritual arsenal.* Therefore, it is wise to remain in a prayerful attitude, sensitive to the leading of the Spirit. That way, we are ready to act upon opportunities that He provides to honor Him with our words by praying for someone in need.

HOW CAN WE USE OUR WORDS TO HONOR GOD?

Controlling the way in which we speak is for many the most difficult discipline of all. God encourages us to control our mouth because ultimately we suffer if we do not. Also, our cross, cruel or insensitive words have the potential of leaving a path of untold relational wreckage, as I said earlier.

I mentioned giving praise to God as one way in which we can use our words to honor God. Instead of speaking evil words, curses and lies, we can make the same choice that David made, to sing of the goodness of our God:

16 But as for me, I shall sing of Thy strength;
**   Yes, I shall joyfully sing of Thy lovingkindness**
**   in the morning,**
**   For Thou hast been my stronghold,...**
                                        —Psalm 59

Practically speaking, just what does this mean? In any situation or circumstance of life, we have a choice as to how we will respond. We can bemoan our plight and speak endlessly of how unjustly we have been treated, or we can focus on the source of our strength and hope, as we see the Psalmist doing in the preceding verse.

When you read the Psalms, keep in mind that King David was not always a king nor was he born into a place of grandeur. He began as an inconsequential shepherd boy, considered to be the least of his brothers. Even after Samuel had prophetically anointed him as king, it was still many years and many hardships later before he saw the fulfillment of that prophecy (1 Sam. 16:6-14). A number of the Psalms were written by David while he was being pursued in the wilderness by Saul, who was seeking his life in a jealous rage! Yet in the midst of such trouble, David chose to sing:

4 Behold, God is my helper;
**   The Lord is the sustainer of my soul.**
                                        —Psalm 54

Perhaps you are facing some trying circumstances right now. How do you apply this? Watch over your heart with all diligence and guard the words that come out of your mouth. Make an active *choice* to focus on what you know to be true—that God is bigger than your situation and He is able to see you through it. Your task is to keep your eyes on Him and your words will reflect the source of your trust.

Psalm 150 exhorts everything that has breath to *praise* the Lord. That includes us!

A theme emerged to me in Psalm 50 that has to do with our words. In much of this Psalm, we see that God is not pleased with the sacrifices of the people, although they are sacrificing animals presumably as the law instructs. Evidently this is directed to a people who speak of God's covenant and yet hate discipline and do not walk in righteousness. *Their religion is a sham that is not backed up by their lives.* God further condemns them specifically for the use of their words, which reveals what is really in their hearts, when He says this:

> 19 "You let your mouth loose in evil,
>   And your tongue frames deceit.
> 20 "You sit and speak against your brother;
>   You slander your own mother's son...."
>
> —Psalm 50

God is displeased when we use the words of our mouth in such a disgraceful manner, slandering even our own brother and speaking deceit. In contrast, the same Psalm tells us how we can instead honor God with our words:

> 14 "Offer to God a sacrifice of thanksgiving,
>   And pay your vows to the Most High;...
> 23 "He who offers a sacrifice of thanksgiving
>   honors Me;
>   And to him who orders *his* way *aright*
>   I shall show the salvation of God."
>
> —Psalm 50

When considering the subject of praise and thanksgiving and a passage such as the one we just read, remember what a *sacrifice* is. A sacrifice *costs* you something. It is easy to give thanks for obviously *good* things and blessings in our lives. I believe that offering to God a *sacrifice of thanksgiving* means choosing to thank Him even in the midst of circumstances that may not look so favorable.

Ultimately, a sacrifice of praise is a gift to yourself, as it refocuses your attention in the most beneficial place it can be—on the Lord and His sufficiency to meet your every need. You may not understand some of the things that life brings right now, but acknowledging that He is bigger and greater than whatever you are facing has a way of setting your perspective aright. As a result, there comes a hope and a peace that surpasses understanding.

When my late husband, James McKeever, passed away of a heart attack (his fifth) in 1995, circumstantially life looked pretty bleak. Yet even in the midst of those initial few shocked days and weeks of numbness and the grief of such a deep loss, I found tremendous solace and strength in singing songs of thanksgiving to God. As I chose to focus my attention in this way, God met me by reminding me that His promises are true and that He is trustworthy, no matter what comes. Your situation may be quite different than mine, but the equation is still the same.

In the following verses, the Psalmist likewise uses His tongue to extol the goodness of the Lord and all that He has done:

> 16 Come *and* hear, all who fear God,
>   And I will tell of what He has done for my soul.
> 17 I cried to Him with my mouth,
>   And He was extolled with my tongue.
>   —Psalm 66

I include these examples to spark your thinking as to positive ways you might use your words. In Biblical times, stories were often passed on to future generations orally. God explicitly commanded the Hebrew people to tell of His miracles of deliverance from generation to generation. Hearing such inspiring stories, such as the miraculous deliverance of the children of Israel out of Egypt, builds faith and expectation that God can rescue us as well from whatever challenges come our way.

In Psalm 71, an old man prays for deliverance. It sounds like he is ready and willing to testify of God's blessings in his life to anyone who will listen (verses 14-22). He concludes by declaring that he will use his mouth to shout for joy and to sing praises to God, his redeemer:

> **23 My lips will shout for joy when I sing praises to Thee;**
> **And my soul, which Thou has redeemed.**
> **24 My tongue also will utter Thy righteousness all day long...**
> **—Psalm 71**

This Psalmist says he will speak of the righteousness of God "all day long." This sounds to me like it was his goal and aim to honor God with his words at all times.

We have already touched briefly on the fact that David chose to give abundant thanks and praise with his mouth. This can be seen throughout the book of Psalms. Here is another instance:

> **30 With my mouth I will give thanks abundantly to the Lord;**
> **And in the midst of many I will praise Him.**
> **—Psalm 109**

Sometimes it is helpful for us to make declarations to our soul of what we intend to do. Resolve is the first step toward follow through.

Remember, quite a number of the Psalms were written when David was in significant distress, as you may be in your present situation. His life was not an easy one, yet he chose to make these declarations:

> 1   **I will exalt you, my God the King;**
>   **I will praise your name for ever and ever.**
> 2   **Every day I will praise you and extol your name**
>   **for ever and ever....**
> 6   **They will tell of the power of your awesome**
>   **works, and I will proclaim your great deeds.**
> 7   **They will celebrate your abundant goodness**
>   **and joyfully sing of your righteousness....**
> 21   **My mouth will speak in praise of the LORD....**
>   **—Psalm 145,** *NIV*

Here we see that David repeatedly *purposed to glorify the Lord with his mouth.* We too can make the decision and assertion that we will use our words to bless the Lord, to speak the praise of the Lord, to recount His abundant goodness and to speak of His awesome acts in our lives. In verse 4 of the same Psalm, David said that one nation would praise God's works to another and declare His mighty acts. Each of us can determine now to be a person who will proclaim God's faithfulness and awesome acts with the words of our mouth.

The book of Titus is another that abounds with references to words. It says that rebellious men who are empty talkers and deceivers must be silenced, for they are upsetting whole families, teaching things that they should not teach, motivated by sordid gain (Titus 1:10-11). In contrast, the author gives Titus this instruction concerning his words:

> **1 But as for you, speak the things which are fitting for sound doctrine.**
>
> **—Titus 2**

He further says that, rather than being malicious gossips, older women ought to encourage and edify the younger women with their words (Titus 2:3-5). Young people growing up are looking for role models. God planned it that way. Young men are tremendously influenced by the example of grown men they respect, and the same is true with young women who model themselves after grown women they admire. These verses in Titus serve to emphasize just how much power women can have with their words in shaping young lives. In today's society, an angry, resentful older woman can sow seeds of malcontent and distrust of all men, for example, by bitter words that reflect her own unresolved, unhealed pain issues. Such poisonous seeds can detrimentally affect the entire life of a young person seeking direction and guidance, as well as affecting generations to come.

KEEPING YOUR WORD

The Scriptures make it clear that our words are very important in God's sight, as we have seen thus far. It used to be that if a man gave his word on something, it was "as good as a bond"—that is to say, as good as a written pledge or contract. If someone gave his word on something, you were able to count on it; he was honor-bound to keep it. A firm handshake often sealed the deal. We have drifted away from these values as a society, but

God has not. He does not lightly regard a vow given either to Himself or to another person.

This may have originated from the command of the Lord given through Moses that a man should not violate his word or vow, but treat it as a binding commitment:

> **2 "If a man makes a vow to the Lord, or takes an oath to bind himself with a binding obligation, he shall not violate his word; he shall do according to all that proceeds out of his mouth."**
>
> **—Numbers 30**

This is pretty strong and clear-cut: a man should *do according to all that he says he will do.* Put differently, he should *keep his word.* Keeping our word is one way we can mirror the character of God, who always keeps His word.

Numbers 30 deals with the laws of vows. Much of the chapter addresses a woman's vows. If her father (while she is in her father's household) or her husband annuls any vows she has made, then they shall not stand. However, if he says nothing when he hears of it, then she is bound by every vow and obligation she has made. Even if it was a rash statement of her lips, it shall stand (Num. 30:3-8). *Apparently, the keeping of one's word is a very important thing to the Lord.*

The words of our mouth spoken in a vow are *powerful.* In short, vows are not to be made lightly, and if you make one, you should be careful to keep it.

> **21 "When you make a vow to the LORD your God, you shall not delay to pay it, for it would be sin in you, and the LORD your God will surely require it of you.**
> **22 "However, if you refrain from vowing, it would not be sin in you.**

23 "You shall be careful to perform what goes out from your lips, just as you have voluntarily vowed to the LORD your God, what you have promised...."
—Deuteronomy 23

What that means to me is that if you say you are going to meet someone at a certain time, you would go out of your way, if necessary, to be certain to do so. Moreover, you plan your life accordingly so that you are able to fulfill the commitments you have made. If you commit to leading a group at church, only true illness or a dire emergency would prevent you from keeping your word. Even then, the honorable thing would be to call and make arrangements for someone to take your place, if at all possible, should you be unable to keep your commitment. In other words, you don't leave people hanging on your promises, wondering whether or not they can count on you. You prove yourself to be reliable and true to your word.

Jesus reemphasized the importance of keeping our word in the New Testament, when He said:

33 "Again, you have heard that the ancients were told, 'YOU SHALL NOT MAKE FALSE VOWS, BUT SHALL FULFILL YOUR VOWS TO THE LORD.'...

37 "But let your statement be, 'Yes, yes' *or* 'No, no'; and anything beyond these is of evil...."
—Matthew 5

Jesus went so far as to label anything short of keeping one's word as being evil! He made it clear that our "yes" should really mean "yes" and our "no" should really mean "no." People should know that we will stand by our word. This is important with our children, too. Children have a way of wearing down their parents. They may get

a "no" the first three or four times. Yet they quickly learn
that if they keep badgering their parents long enough,
when the parent is exhausted and resolve is worn down,
sometimes they will give in. Succumbing to the pressure
can become *easier* than standing by their word. Letting
your kids know that your "yes" means "yes" and your
"no" means "no" is a very good example for them and one
they are likely to emulate.

I view the keeping of your word as an important part
of your spiritual armor, as it is crucial to being a person
of integrity. Integrity involves being dependable and
trustworthy, among other things. Hence, being a person
whose word is *reliable* is a potent testimony.

BE SLOW TO SPEAK

James, the brother of Jesus, admonishes us to be *slow
to speak*.

**19 ...But let everyone be quick to hear, slow to
speak *and* slow to anger;...**
—James 1

Most likely, every one of us can recall instances when
we spoke without thinking and later regretted something
we had said. Perhaps our thoughtless comment hurt
someone else or displayed our ignorance on a subject.
Oftentimes arguments are started because we rush in
where angels fear to tread, not weighing our words before
we utter them.

Recently, a friend called to see if I was planning to
go to an upcoming Ladies Cycle Campout weekend.
Without any forethought as to how it could be interpreted,
I happened to ask her whether she had a tent mate yet,

neglecting to give her the whole picture of my situation. Excitedly, she responded that she did not and would love to share a tent! I then had to further explain that I had invited a couple of new ladies and had yet to hear back from them, so I could not commit to sharing a tent until I had heard from them. A gracious woman, she covered her disappointment well, but my ill-planned comment had taken a toll in hurt feelings, nonetheless.

James' admonition to be slow to speak holds great wisdom. Just what do you think it means to be "quick to hear"? It sounds to me like he is putting an emphasis on the *listening* part of communication. Have you *really heard* what the other guy is saying, before you jump in with a retort or an attempt to make your point? Many of us are so concerned with formulating our reply in our minds while someone else is still speaking that we miss a lot of what is being said. We may ostensibly be "listening," but are we really *hearing*?

Then, when we do speak, have we considered the impact our words will have or are we speaking off-the-cuff, possibly responding in anger, pride or defensiveness with a remark we will later wish we could retract? Yes, I believe James was right—one way we can honor God is by being *"quick to hear and slow to speak."*

A TIME TO SPEAK

According to Proverbs, there is a time to use words for good, in defending the rights of the unfortunate, the afflicted, and the needy:

8 Open your mouth for the dumb,
For the rights of all the unfortunate.

9 Open your mouth, judge righteously, and defend
the rights of the afflicted and needy.
—Proverbs 31

Later in the same chapter, Solomon describes an
excellent wife as one who *"opens her mouth in wisdom"*
and has *"the teaching of kindness on her tongue"* (Prov.
31:26). He gives us this further piece of sound advice
concerning our words in an earlier Proverb:

3 The one who guards his mouth preserves his life;
The one who opens wide his lips comes to ruin.
—Proverbs 13

Most likely, all of us can bring to mind someone who
is continually "putting his (or her) foot in his
mouth"—that is, speaking rashly or without forethought,
to his own detriment. Maybe this applies to us. We can
be our own worst enemy when we fail to guard our words
wisely!

The good news is that broken promises or hurts from
thoughtless or inconsiderate words *can* be repaired, often
by the same means the damage was done—with words.
Humble, genuinely contrite words of apology when we
make a mistake can be a healing balm to the wound.
Relationships can be strengthened, even through our
failings, if we are quick to admit a mistake and sincerely
say some of the most potent words around: "I'm sorry; I
was wrong. Please forgive me."

Even better is to be more specific. People will
generally perceive that you don't really mean it if an
apology comes across as flippant. Saying something like
the following lets them know that you truly see and
acknowledge your offense and the hurt that it caused:

"I was wrong in what I said. Please forgive me for the hurtful words that I spoke to you."

This clears the page totally and helps immeasurably to heal a wounded heart. As one friend puts it, *"Flowers come from the wallet; words come from the heart."* After thirty years of marriage, he has learned that the best way to soothe his wife's ruffled feathers is with healing words.

THE ART OF BEING HUMAN

None of us is perfect in being able to maintain the spiritual guidelines outlined in these pages. In fact, a verse from James that we read in Chapter 1 stated that we all stumble in many ways. The *New International Version* goes on to say:

> **2   ...If anyone is never at fault in what he says, he is a perfect man, able to keep his whole body in check.**
> **—James 3, *NIV***

The *Amplified Bible* gives further insight, stating how imperfect we all are and how taking control our tongue is a worthy goal, as well as a strong indicator of spiritual maturity and character:

> **2   For we all often stumble *and* fall *and* offend in many things. And if any one does not offend in speech—never says the wrong things—he is a fully developed character *and* a perfect man, able to control his whole body *and* to curb his entire nature.**
> **—James 3, *Amplified***

I am not advocating becoming a religious perfectionist (which is its own debilitating disease), but focusing our attention on using the invaluable gift of speech wisely and being willing to look to God for help as we walk our spiritual path. That is the goal and He will help anyone who begins from that point of yieldedness.

By applying Scriptural principles, the person who stands to gain the most—in experiencing inner peace, the love of others, as well as a healthy love of self—is you. The teachings of Jesus are a wonderful instructional manual for healthy living. Throughout the centuries, the Scriptures have provided a splendid spiritual roadmap on how to maximize the happiness and tranquility that is available to each of us.

OUR SPEECH IS A TESTIMONY

In a portion of his letter to Timothy where he is giving some specific instructions, Paul says, *"in speech, conduct, love, faith and purity, show yourself an example of those who believe"* (1 Tim. 4:12). As well as our actions being an important testimony to others, evidently Paul considered our speech to be a very significant part of the example we give to the world of what it means to be a believer.

Peter admonishes us, if we wish to love life and see good days, to restrain our tongue from speaking evil and our lips from speaking guile (1 Pet. 3:1). John warns us not to speak empty words but to back up our words with action in the form of good deeds (1 John 3:18). Both give good advice, if we wish to honor God with our words.

Isaiah made this amazing statement in the middle of a passage that appears to be prophetic about Jesus:

> 4 **The Lord GOD has given Me the tongue of dis-**
> **ciples,**

> **That I may know how to sustain the weary one with a word....**
>
> **—Isaiah 50**

How wonderful and inspiring to know that we can sustain someone who is weary with a timely word. Life can become a great adventure, if we start looking for daily opportunities to do just that. Your word may bring a smile to the face of another who needed to see a ray of hope. Think of it like spreading sunshine or giving a flower to someone who needs a lift. During one season in my life, I endeavored to invest five minutes every day writing and mailing a card or note of encouragement to someone I knew could use it. Author Dan Millman refers to this kind of "investment" as practicing "random acts of kindness." Even though you may never *see* the payoff, still it is well worth the investment of a few minutes of time.

I suspect we can agree that believing in Jesus is the foundation of our faith. The following verse informs us that confessing our faith *with our mouth* also has significance:

> **9 that if you confess with your mouth Jesus *as* Lord, and believe in your heart that God raised Him from the dead, you shall be saved;...**
>
> **—Romans 10**

The Bible tells us clearly that every knee will bow and every tongue *confess* that Jesus Christ is Lord (Phil. 2:10, 11). We all will confess Him as Lord sooner or later. We can choose to do so *now*, and not be ashamed to call Him our *Lord*. In so doing, we honor God with our words.

SEASONED WITH GRACE

As noted early in this book, God spoke and the world came into being. We are made in our Father's image and we, too, hold creative, life-giving power in our words. I believe we do well if we train ourselves to use them constructively.

In writing to the Christians in Colossae, Paul had this very wise instruction for them concerning their speech. It is equally sound advice for us today:

> **6 Let your speech always be with grace, seasoned, as it were, with salt, so that you may know how you should respond to each person.**
> **—Colossians 4**

Have you ever stopped to think about what it means to let your *"speech always be with grace"?* Grace is unmerited favor. Always speaking with grace would seem to me to entail giving the other person the benefit of the doubt and not retaliating with defensive or angry words, even when you may think they are merited. Can I say that I always do that? Hardly! I'm far from it! In fact, as I read this over, I am reminded of how I sometimes do want to retaliate and "set another person straight," particularly if I perceive an injustice. That seems to be the natural response of our fleshly nature. Grace is a *choice*—and, remember, it means *unmerited favor*. The person to whom you are responding may not *deserve* your kindness in the way you choose to reply. Nonetheless, I believe responding with grace is always a worthy goal.

I think this is one reason people were so impressed with Jesus—He spoke graciously, as we read earlier (Luke 4:22). He did not return evil for evil, with either His words or His deeds. We can make a choice to follow His example in this.

Just this morning I reacted to my husband in a curt, testy fashion, when I perceived what seemed to be an unfair expectation. He called me on it, and I was truly sorry that once again I had given in to responding to him in a thoughtless, ungracious, impatient manner. So many conflicts are a result of nothing but misunderstanding and pride—*"I'm* right, so therefore you must be wrong!" I called him later to say, "I'm sorry for the way I reacted. I was wrong. Please forgive me." It felt so good to know that clear, open channels of communication and mutual appreciation had been restored between us, that nothing stood in the way.

Cleaning up your mistakes is one way to create trust. Having to ask for forgiveness is humbling and may not be easy, especially if you feel as though you have also been mistreated. Maybe you feel as if the wrong against you is greater than any offense you have committed. So what? You are still responsible for cleaning up your own side of the street. If you want to mature spiritually, that is where your attention should be—not on how you were wronged. Despite the difficulty of laying your ego aside (dying to self), it is definitely always worth the effort to seek restoration of a relationship by asking for forgiveness.

Paul wrote some powerful words of instruction to the church at Ephesus about taking charge over their mouths. He said:

> **29 Let no unwholesome word proceed from your mouth, but only such *a word* as is good for edification according to the need *of the moment*, that it may give grace to those who hear.**
> **30 And do not grieve the Holy Spirit of God, by whom you were sealed for the day of redemption.**

31 Let all bitterness and wrath and anger and clamor and slander be put away from you, along with all malice.

32 And be kind to one another, tender-hearted, forgiving each other, just as God in Christ also has forgiven you.

—Ephesians 4

This passage does not say to *manage* bitterness, wrath, and anger but *to get rid of them*. We are not to harbor and nurture these defiling emotions in our hearts. The way to deal with them is through forgiveness[8] which is an integral ingredient in "heart management"—that is, keeping our hearts clean. As we have seen, out of our heart flows the springs of life and our words are a major conduit.

By now it is becoming unmistakably evident that our words carry with them tremendous power for good *or* detriment. The ideas cited in this chapter are just *some* examples of ways in which we can use our tongue in a manner that honors the One who gave us the priceless gift of speech.

And remember—you are a *mighty mouth*.

Chapter 4

POWER UNLEASHED
IN BLESSING

We have discussed some ways to use our words constructively, such as speaking a timely word of encouragement, hope or edification, keeping our word, speaking truth in love, and being sensitive to others in the method of delivery and the timing of what we say. Another very specific positive use of words is in blessing one another. Just as cursing can have a far-reaching negative impact, most of us have no idea of the positive power of the blessing. By "cursing" here, let me distinguish between the use of profanity (bad language or swearing) and literal cursing. What I mean in this context is this:

"To call upon divine or supernatural power to send injury upon; to bring great evil upon."[1]

The chain of effects that is put into motion from an actual curse spoken upon someone can be horrific, both for the curser and the accursed. Do not take lightly the fact that our words carry creative power. Speaking a curse on someone is a damaging and unprofitable use of words. In contrast, blessing means:

"A thing conducive to happiness or welfare."[2]

The Old Testament has many instances of one person blessing another. The power of the blessing was well understood and respected in that day. It was part of the Hebrew culture and practice for fathers to pass on blessings to their sons:

> **20 By faith Isaac blessed Jacob and Esau, even regarding things to come.**
> **21 By faith Jacob, as he was dying, blessed each of the sons of Joseph, and worshiped, leaning on the top of his staff.**
> **—Hebrews 11**

Perhaps most well known is the incident when Isaac is going to bless his first-born son, Esau. Jacob, his younger son, dresses up in Esau's clothes, pretending to be him, in order to receive the blessing of the first-born son. (You can read this story in Genesis 27.)

When Jacob is old, he blesses the two sons of Joseph, Ephraim and Manasseh, crossing his hands to put them on their heads (see Gen. 48:14-20). The major blessing was believed to come through the right hand, which was traditionally placed on the head of the first-born. Joseph tries to correct his father, pointing out that Manasseh is the first-born. But Jacob refuses and says that the younger brother will be greater than the first-born and his descendants will become a multitude of nations.

Just before his death, Jacob calls together all of his twelve sons. The first 27 verses of Genesis 29 itemize the specific blessing that he gives to each of his sons, as summarized in this verse:

> **28 All these are the twelve tribes of Israel, and this is what their father said to them when he blessed them. He blessed them, every one with the blessing appropriate to him.**
>
> **—Genesis 49**

There are many other examples that illustrate our Old Testament forefathers' familiarity with and respect for the blessing. Moses, Aaron and Joshua are all recorded as blessing people (Ex. 39:43; Lev. 9:22-23; Josh. 14:13; 22:6-7). Scripture records that King David blesses the people in the name of the Lord of hosts, and then returns to bless his household (2 Sam. 6:18, 20). King Solomon speaks a beautiful blessing on the assembly of Israel (1 Kings 8:14, 55-61).

The people and the elders bless Boaz after his statement of commitment to take Ruth as his wife and to care for her and to raise up the name of her deceased husband (Ruth 4:10-12). Undoubtedly, this gracious blessing makes Ruth feel loved, accepted and welcomed by the people of that land.

In the New Testament, Jesus takes the children in His arms, lays hands on them and blesses them (Mark 10:16). In addition, *we* are instructed to give a blessing (1 Pet. 3:8-9; Rom. 12:14).

Hopefully, you can begin to see what I mean when I say that the concept of blessing runs throughout Scripture. It was a very common and regular practice. Have you ever considered that perhaps the Lord would like it to be part of our lives, as well?

THE BLESSING IN OUR LIVES

A number of years ago at a particular local community function, I noticed that one of my neighbors seemed especially cool, as though she had a problem with me. I could not recollect anything I had done to offend her, but there was a decided standoffishness or lack of warmth from an otherwise very bubbly, friendly person. This bothered me for some time. I considered taking matters into my own hands (operating in the flesh) and confronting her about it, because of the discomfort I was feeling about the apparent, but inexplicable, chasm between us.

I pass by this couples' driveway and mailbox quite often when I go for walks along our country road. I began speaking a blessing on them, laying a hand on their mailbox when I walked by. This went on for some time, then I ran into them at a fire fighter's fund-raiser, one of our yearly community functions. Lo and behold, an amazing transformation had taken place. It was as if I were speaking to a different person. The woman was very friendly and we chatted for some time, even making plans for an activity together that we both enjoy.

The healing of whatever offense had blighted our relationship, I believe, was attributable to the power of the blessing. (I never did find out what the problem had been, and it really doesn't matter.)

Consider a relationship in your life that has been damaged and needs healing and restoration—whether or not the damage was due to some fault of yours or to unknown causes. From personal experience, I suggest that you guard your heart by keeping your own hurts and resentments in check. Then start blessing that individual. There is no telling what miracles may unfold in your life when you choose to employ this spiritual principle, no

matter how gloomy the relationship may appear circumstantially.

A very well-known and loved passage is the following one, when the Lord speaks to Moses instructing him
about how to have the priesthood bless the sons of Israel:

> **23 "Speak to Aaron and to his sons, saying, 'Thus
> you shall bless the sons of Israel. You shall say to
> them:**
> **24 The LORD bless you, and keep you;**
> **25 The LORD make His face shine on you,**
> **And be gracious to you;**
> **26 The LORD lift up His countenance on you,**
> **And give you peace,'**
> **27 "So they shall invoke My name on the sons of
> Israel, and I then will bless them."**
>
> **—Numbers 6**

Verse 27 makes it clear that the Lord is the one who
does the blessing and all blessings ultimately flow from
Him, but on occasions, He wants man's involvement.
Aaron and his sons are actually *commanded* to bless the
sons of Israel. In this case, the vehicle or conduit of the
blessing is the priests.

The New Testament states that Jesus Christ makes
those who believe in Him to be *"a kingdom, priests to His
God and Father"* (Rev. 1:5-6). As priests in Jesus Christ,
I believe there is tremendous good unleashed as we pass
on His blessings, at the direction and leading of His Spirit.

Peter was one of Jesus' closest disciples. In writing
to the Christians scattered abroad, in summation, he
instructs them to do a number of things: be harmonious,
sympathetic, brotherly, kind-hearted and humble in Spirit,
not returning evil for evil or insult for insult, *but giving
blessing instead* (1 Pet. 3:8-10). He eloquently admon-

ishes believers to use their words to speak *blessing* instead of evil. He says that one who would like to love life and see good days should refrain from speaking evil and guile. Choosing to bless is a much more desirable response than exchanging insults with someone. That is never productive and generally only causes hurt and stirs up anger.

Once again, it seems quite clear here that one of the things God desires of His children is that we actively give blessings. As we do, it magically seems to open a gateway for us to receive blessing.

HOW TO BLESS?

What does it mean to bless someone? Very simply put, it is earnestly speaking the good things over an individual that you want to see in his life. Among the meanings *Webster's* gives for blessing is this:

"A thing conducive to happiness or welfare."[3]

As Jack and I were discussing how we would describe what a blessing is, he came up with this definition that I find particularly concise and descriptive:

"A blessing is an invocation of God's presence and power."

I heard Bill Lignon preach a sermon years ago on the power of the blessing. He shared how God told him that he was going to build a church by blessing the people. As he began to bless the congregation at the end of each service, with success in their businesses, happy home lives and financial prosperity, the church began to grow by leaps and bounds. People started sharing with one another and others would come to the church wanting to receive that blessing. Parents began to bless their children, whose grades subsequently improved remarkably. Marriages began to prosper and businesses solidify.

Another example of the power unleashed by the practice of blessing involved a young girl who had a problem with bed wetting at an age where this generally would no longer be an issue. One night her parents blessed her as she slept. They blessed her with control over her bladder and many other good things that came to their minds that they wanted for her. She never wet the bed again! One young boy was having nightmares and would wake up screaming. After he went to sleep one night, his father entered his bedroom and blessed him with a peaceful sleep and a heart free from fear. The results were astounding. The boy stopped having the nightmares.

A family I know had four children who were school age at the time. The parents got into the practice of blessing their children before they went to school with clear minds, concentration in their studies, good behavior, healthy relationships with classmates, happy memories and other good things. It made such a difference in their schoolwork that before long the children did not want to leave for school without first having their blessing!

A dear friend, Dr. Mary Ruth Swope, wrote a small book entitled, *Bless Your Children Every Day*. In it, she addresses the subject of blessing your children and your grandchildren. Perhaps this concept of blessing your children is new to you. Here are her 49 chapter titles, which may give you inspiration and ideas, as you consider blessing your own children.

Abilities
Abundance
Angels
Assurance
Authority
Children
Clear Direction
A Controlled Tongue
Courage
Creativity
Deliverance
Eternal Life
Eyes to See
Faith
Favor
Fear of the Lord
A Free Spirit
Good Health
A Good Wife
Hands that Bless
Happiness
Holiness
Holy Spirit
Hope
Humility

Joy
Listening Ears
Longevity
Love
A Loving Husband
Mercy
The Mind of Christ
Ministry
Miracles
Obedience
Peace
Pleasant Words
Pleasing Personality
Praise
Promotion
Prosperity
Protection
Provision
Safety
Spiritual Power
Strength
Success
Trust
Wisdom

These are just for inspiration to release your own creativity, as you ask the Holy Spirit to guide your heart, your words and your thoughts. He will put in your mind specific blessings that apply to your loved ones.

One of Mary Ruth's grandchildren wrote the following about the personal reward of having received spoken blessings as she was growing up:

During the times when I was most overwrought, she would draw me close and hold me, asking God to pour out the oil of joy over my mind and heart. Little did I know that these prayers would soon move me from restlessness to peace. Her words stimulated my mind and settled on my then-broken spirit in a way I had never experienced before nor believed could be humanly possible.[4]

As you can tell, these childhood blessings brought healing and hope. Here is an example of one of the complete blessings in Dr. Swope's book:

STRENGTH
In the Name of Jesus Christ:
You will be strong and make your boast in the Lord for He is your Rock. He is your High Tower.
He is the source of all your energy, and He alone can give power to the faint and increase strength when you have none. Even in your youth, there may be times when you feel weak, but your strength will be renewed as you wait upon the Lord. You will be empowered to soar like an eagle. You will run and not be weary. You will walk and not collapse along the way.
Call upon Him to give you strength sufficient for every task. May your strength equal your days.[5]

Mary Ruth makes this observation: *"Your words of blessing are energized by the power of God when you speak them."*
Scriptures can be used very effectively in blessing someone. The most powerful and life-giving words ever spoken were and are God's words.
Making a practice of blessing your children, your spouse, friends and others with whom you come into

contact can have astounding results. They will be enriched, and so will you. A husband and wife can develop and nurture a habit of blessing each other the last thing they do at night before they go to sleep. What a precious and cherished expression that can become, as well as a pleasant way to drift off to sleep!

CHOOSING TO BLESS

I think it is an impressive and weighty thing for parents to speak a blessing on their children when they marry. Even if you have children who are already married, it is never inappropriate to go back and speak your words of blessing on their marriage and their family.

Blessing for patience, endurance, strength, opportunities to be used by the Lord, and joy are things that we all need at any time. Jesus Himself exhorts us to *bless with our lips*, even those who curse and mistreat us!

> **28 "...bless those who curse you, pray for those who mistreat you...."**
>
> —**Luke 6**

Speaking a blessing on someone who mistreats us isn't necessarily our first response after a perceived offense or threat. In the flesh, we typically want to retaliate instead. But, I cannot stress enough that when we choose to bless our enemies, we unleash something powerful in the heavenly realm.

I have the utmost respect for the late Richard Wurmbrand, former Romanian pastor and author of the powerful little book *Tortured for Christ*. He was imprisoned for his faith for fourteen years in Romania. He said that he made it through his days of torture by praying for and blessing his tormentors. Had he not done that, he relates, he is not sure that he could have kept his sanity.

Paul echoes the teaching of Christ on this matter when he writes to the Roman Christians. Ultimately, the church in Rome would become a very persecuted church. He instructs them to:

> **14 Bless those who persecute you; bless and curse not....**
>
> **17 Never pay back evil for evil to anyone. Respect what is right in the sight of all men.**
> **18 If possible, so far as it depends on you, be at peace with all men.**
> **19 Never take your own revenge, beloved, but leave room for the wrath *of God,* for it is written, "VENGEANCE IS MINE, I WILL REPAY," says the Lord.**
> **20 "BUT IF YOUR ENEMY IS HUNGRY, FEED HIM, AND IF HE IS THIRSTY, GIVE HIM A DRINK; FOR IN SO DOING YOU WILL HEAP BURNING COALS UPON HIS HEAD."**
> **21 Do not be overcome by evil, but overcome evil with good.**
>
> **—Romans 12**

Paul develops this concept of blessing further by saying never to pay back evil for evil, but to actually *overcome evil with good.* In our day and culture, the expression in verse 20 about heaping burning coals upon the head of your enemy can be a little confusing. We might think, "Yes, be nice to him and God will get him!" Yet that is still a vengeful attitude.

In the day this was written, fire was a very precious commodity. You could share the warmth of your fire with another by taking some of your burning coals and placing them in a firepan which your neighbor (or enemy) could then take home to easily start his own fire. With that understanding, this comment makes much more sense in context. That is, we are not to pay back evil for evil, but instead we are to *bless* our enemy, both in *word and deed*. In so doing, we overcome evil with good.

There is no doubt that it takes faith to bless those who are our enemies, particularly in times of persecution! Actually, it takes faith to give any blessing, as we read earlier in Hebrews:

> **20 By faith Isaac blessed Jacob and Esau, even regarding things to come.**
> **21 By faith Jacob, as he was dying, blessed each of the sons of Joseph...**
>
> **—Hebrews 11**

Perhaps some people come to mind whom you would like to bless, but you don't know how to go about it. Maybe they are miles away, such as grown children or other loved ones. I believe that a written blessing can also have an impact, as well as one spoken over the telephone or in person. The Holy Spirit is more than able to quicken (make alive) the written word when it is read. As you are writing down the good things that you would like to happen to your loved one, you can be speaking the words vocally, releasing blessings in the heavenly realm. In the name of Jesus Christ, perhaps you want to bless the individual on your heart with health, with a long and productive life, with good and caring friendships and loving relationships, with freedom from worry and with financial security, for example.

A THOUGHT TO CONSIDER
—THE REALM OF THE SPIRIT

A friend who reviewed this manuscript, Debbie Horton, shared this interesting insight that she received while reading it:

> Who is our enemy? Yes indeed, it's Satan. Scripture tells us that Satan is Prince of the Air. What do our words travel through? (I hear your "Aha!")
>
> When our words are negative, they meet no resistance. When our words are positive, they drag and grind. This friction causes both heat and fire in the spiritual realm of the air.
>
> Scripture also tells us that evil in family lines lasts for four generations, but *blessings endure for seven generations.* If a generation is 40 years, then when we bless our children, that blessing will carry on for 280 years!

This gives further weight to the potential power of the blessing. If you were to bless your children with a strong spiritual walk, for example, that blessing could pass on to future generations as a mantle of protection in ways we cannot even begin to comprehend.

When Debbie spoke of positive words creating heat and fire in the spiritual realm, I had the mental image of sparks from friction creating *light.* We know that God is *light,* as opposed to the kingdom of *darkness,* over which the Prince of the Air currently reigns. I repeat, our words are a powerful spiritual weapon. I certainly want to be one who spreads light.

Right now, dear reader, I bless you with a calm spirit and a serene receptivity of what God is speaking to you personally in this moment. I bless you with fulfillment of your dreams and the ability to lay hold of the fullness of who you are in God and of His great love for you. I bless you with joy, a deep abiding peace, and an ever teachable, humble spirit. I bless you with discernment to glean from these pages the message that is for your life today, in the name of Jesus Christ our Lord.

Chapter 5

AN "APPRECIATION
HAPPENING"!

A few years after I gave my heart and life to the Lord
as a teenager, I was part of a youth group that met Sunday
evenings in a Baptist church. One evening, the youth
leader announced that we were going to have what he
termed an "Appreciation Happening." I listened with
interest as he described what he meant.

We were to form a large circle with our chairs. Then
we would take turns progressively going around the circle,
highlighting each individual, one at a time. Everyone in
the circle would have an opportunity to say something that
he or she appreciated about each of the other teenagers
present. It was not mandatory to comment on every
person (or on any, for that matter), but we were encouraged to include as many people as we honestly could. It
was an excellent opportunity to turn our thoughts to the
positive characteristics that we could see in the various
people within our youth group.

Even those who were not the most popular or charis-
matic in personality had good qualities, when we put our
energies into focusing on the good, rather than the offen-

sive or less appealing characteristics or behavior. It gave us a unique opportunity to see one another in a new light. Comments were made and appreciation of attributes expressed that, in some cases, had never been voiced before. It was a tremendously encouraging experience for all involved, and one that I have never forgotten.

Interestingly, a CNN Headline News report June 1, 2000 stated that fellow students described the two perpetrators of the tragic 1999 Columbine school shooting as "loners." This was one of the observations other Columbine teens (including some of the wounded) made as they sought to make sense of the catastrophe and to pass on what they had learned to students in other school districts. They encouraged students to reach out with greetings to such teens. In retrospect, they wondered if a show of friendship to those two boys might have made a difference.

Since the time of my own high school "Appreciation Happening" experience, on a smaller scale, I have tried the same thing with groups of just four or five people. It has always been an edifying experience. All too often in life, people focus on the negative, unfortunately sometimes to the near exclusion of the positive.

It is my belief that it is a healthy exercise to occasionally set aside time to take inventory of the things we see in others that are positive and worthy of our appreciation. Then it may be valuable for us to go out of our way to actually express that genuine appreciation verbally to that person. Sometimes those who need to hear it the most are those closest to us—like a spouse, a child, a sibling, a parent or a best friend. These are the ones we seem to easily take for granted.

I am convinced that you cannot go wrong in speaking good words. Most of us are bombarded with enough of

the other kind all day long that a good word spoken from
the heart can be a refreshment to the soul, a healing balm
to a wounded or dejected spirit. Proverbs 15 puts it this
way:

> **4 A soothing tongue is a tree of life,...**
> **—Proverbs 15**

What a phrase—*a tree of life!* Even that analogy
carries with it the connotation of *strength* and *sustenance.*

WORDS CAN
STRENGTHEN AND EDIFY

Sometimes all of us just need to hear a good word.

> **25 Anxiety in the heart of a man weighs it down.**
> **But a good word makes it glad.**
> **—Proverbs 12**

Solomon speaks volumes of truth with this simple
verse of contrast. He knew well the power of a good
word to make the heart glad and to dispel the weighty
pressure of anxieties.

Isaiah recognized the power that was in his tongue, as
we see in this verse we read earlier:

> **4 The Lord God has given Me the tongue of dis-**
> **ciples,**
> **That I may know how to sustain the weary one**
> **with a word....**
> **—Isaiah 50**

What an awesome privilege we have to be able to
sustain, with an encouraging word, someone who is weary
in the battle, perhaps about to give up. I hope that by

now you are really getting the idea of what I mean when I say *we hold the power of life and death in our tongue* (Prov. 18:21). The right words spoken to someone who has run out of hope can reinspire and provide the needed strength to go on.

HOW YOU SPEAK IS AS IMPORTANT AS *WHAT* YOU SAY

Words can be a very precise tool to communicate our thoughts and feelings to someone else. Although we can never be absolutely sure that the person listening is receiving exactly the same message that we are trying to give, words still allow us to communicate very detailed information, feelings and subtleties of meaning quite specifically. The more vocabulary in a language, the more specific the communication can be in shades of possible interpretation.

Even though this is true, researchers have concluded that the actual *content* of what we say to someone else is only about 30 percent of the message the other person receives! The rest is communicated by a whole host of other factors, such as the tone of our voice, inflection, eye contact, body language and so on. People can generally tell whether or not you are sincere in what you are saying, because of these unspoken indicators.

Words spoken in anger, for example, are easy to distinguish from words spoken in gentleness and love. Even a dog or cat can tell when you are angry by the tenor of your voice. Thus, tone and attitude are equally as important as the specific words you utter. Together these other factors comprise a significant part of the message conveyed.

The following study shows measurable differences can be related to the way in which we choose to speak:

> *Speak slowly and softly.* A 1990 study reported what happened when participants were asked to discuss anger-arousing events using three different voice styles: fast and loud; slow and soft; and normal conversational tone. Men and women both had a much higher rise in blood pressure and heart rate, *and they felt much more anger,* when they spoke in the fast/loud style compared to their normal speaking voice. These same people had much lower pulse and blood pressure readings *and felt significantly less anger* when they spoke slowly and softly.
>
> When discussing hot topics, practicing speaking more softly and slower than usual will reduce your frustrations and improve the odds you won't withdraw from the conversation.[1]

We saw earlier that Jesus spoke "gracious words." Other passages in Scripture reveal that He spoke with compassion, authority and love. In seeking to honor God with our words, it is also advisable that we give heed to *how* we are coming across and affecting others, as well as the actual content of our words.

GET CONTROL
OF YOUR TONGUE

In the following excerpt, Rabbi Joseph Telushkin poses an intriguing challenge:

> Over the past decade, whenever I have lectured throughout the country on the powerful, and often nega-tive, impact of words, I have asked audiences if they can

go for twenty-four hours without saying any unkind words about, or to, anybody.

Invariably, a minority of listeners raise their hands signifying "yes," some laugh, and quite a large number call out, "no!"

I respond by saying, "Those who can't answer 'yes' must recognize that you have a serious problem. If you cannot go for twenty-four hours without drinking liquor, you are addicted to alcohol. If you cannot go for twenty-four hours without smoking, you are addicted to nicotine. Similarly, if you cannot go for twenty-four hours without saying unkind words about others, then you have lost control over your tongue."

How can I compare the harm done by a bit of gossip or a few unpleasant words to the damage caused by alcohol and smoking? Well, just think about your own life for a minute. Unless you, or someone dear to you, has been the victim of terrible physical violence, chances are the worst pains you have suffered in life have come from words used cruelly—from ego-destroying criticism, excessive anger, sarcasm, public and private humiliation, hurtful nicknames, betrayal of secrets, rumors and malicious gossip.[2]

The author of this article further proposes a National "Speak No Evil" Day. He describes a resolution to establish such a day requesting that the President issue a proclamation calling on the American people to:

 — eliminate all hurtful and unfair talk for twenty-four hours;
 — transmit negative information only when necessary;
 — monitor and regulate how they speak to others;
 — strive to keep anger under control;
 — argue fairly, and not allow disputes to degenerate into name-calling or other forms of verbal abuse;

— and speak about others with the same kindness and fairness that they wish others to exercise when speaking about them.

A "Speak No Evil" Day would plant the seed of a more permanent shift in our consciousness. It would hopefully touch everyone—from journalists, politicians, activists, teachers, ministers, and businessmen to mothers, fathers, brothers, sisters, sons and daughters....

It will be a day when people will use words that heal others' emotional wounds, not those that inflict them.[3]

This may be an idealistic and unattainable goal, but each of us *can* take individual responsibility for our own speech.

By now we clearly see that we can either edify or tear down others by what we say and that the words which we speak are important to the Lord. Following are listed some nouns that have to do with words. Which ones would you say apply to you, as something that you practice regularly?

Checklist

accusation	appreciation
backbiting	blessing
complaining	encouragement
criticizing	edifying
cursing	inspiring
gossip	instructing
nagging	motivating
slander	praise

If you find yourself relating to some terms in the first column and not relating to some in the second column,... "Houston, we have a problem!" It might be food for some introspective thought and prayer. Perhaps the Lord is wanting to speak to you about letting Him be Lord over your mouth and the words that you speak. Like anything else in life, discipline in this area requires some effort and a decisive application of principles we want to be characteristic of our lives.

King David must have realized the significance of his words, for he sets an admirable goal for himself not to sin with the words of his mouth.

> **3 ...I have resolved that my mouth will not sin.**
> **—Psalm 17, *NIV***

He also prays for the Lord to set a guard over his lips.

> **3 Set a guard, O Lord, over my mouth;**
> **Keep watch over the door of my lips.**
> **—Psalm 141**

We would do well to daily pray this same prayer and likewise purpose not to sin with the words that come out of our mouth.

In his letter to Titus, Paul urges the young men to be *"sound in speech which is beyond reproach"* (Titus 2:6-8). In this way, he says that the opponent will be put to shame having nothing bad to say about us. Most of us have a good ways to go in order to have it said of us that our speech is *"beyond reproach."*

Jesus said that He did not speak on His own initiative, but in obedience to the commandment of His Father who told Him what to say (John 12:49-50). Imagine if we were to truly wait on the Lord about what and when to speak, as Jesus did. It would undoubtedly clean up a lot of the idle, careless, hurtful and thoughtless words that we sometimes are guilty of speaking.

The good news is that now is a great day to determine that you will purpose to glorify God in your speech. This very moment, you and I can begin to pray, as David did, that the words of our mouth will be acceptable in God's sight:

> **14 Let the words of my mouth and the meditation of my heart**
> **Be acceptable in Thy sight, O LORD, my rock and my Redeemer.**
> **—Psalm 19**

Plainly and simply, it is honoring to the Lord when we seek to glorify Him in our words. In addition, having our tongue under His control also harnesses an incredibly powerful tool for good.

During an interview aired in April of 2000, basketball legend Michael Jordon shared how the television minidrama, "Roots," aroused all kinds of emotions in him. The historic injustices to blacks made him want to retaliate. He cited his mother's words to him; she told him to rise above it. He credited his parents and their positive influence on him for the success he became in his endeavor of choice. His mother's simple but profound words, "Rise above it, Michael," forcibly affected the direction and future success of this then-budding young athlete.

TO GOD BE THE GLORY

We have seen that our words can be a weapon that either causes hurt and devastation or brings healing and help. How we choose to use our speech is up to us individually. A decision to honor God with your words can revolutionize your life and relationships—*that's how powerful the spoken word can be.*

As with any area of our life or behavior, bringing our tongue under control of the Holy Spirit is *a process*, something we approach one day at a time. It begins with a conscious effort to keep our heart pure and to watch our words. May our heavenly Father grant grace to both you and me, as we together endeavor to let the words of our mouth be acceptable in His sight and to be used as a tool to positively impact others within our personal sphere of influence.

The cartoon character, "Mighty Mouse," always sang out, "Here I come to save the day!" Rather fitting, I think—good, helpful, wholesome words to the rescue! Remember, you are a *mighty mouth.* Here come His words through you to save the day!

FOOTNOTES

Quotes

[1]Ron Williams, "Being Pentecostal—Part II," *Foursquare World Advance,* P.O. Box 26902, 1910 West Sunset Blvd, Ste. 200, Los Angeles, CA 90026, May/June 2000, p. 2.

Chapter 1

[1]Paul Hegstrom, *"Cherished—Embracing Your First Love"* Life Skills International, P.O. Box 31227, Aurora, CO 80041.

[2]If you are interested in learning more about this wonderful story of triumph and healing, contact the address on the last page of this book for some terrific resources available, including a moving, Emmy-nominated CBS movie made about Paul and Judy's struggles and recovery from a life marred by years of domestic violence.

[3]Will Carleton, "The First Settler's Story," *Harper's New Monthly Magazine,* Vol. 63, Issue 373, Harper & Bros. New York, June 1881, p. 87-91.

Chapter 2

[1]Rick Joyner, *Epic Battle of the Last Days,* MorningStar Publications, Charlotte, North Carolina, 1995, p. 31.

[2]Rabbi Joseph Telushkin, "Words That Hurt, Words That Heal: How To Choose Words Wisely And Well," *Imprimis,* Vol. 25, Number 1, Hillsdale College, Hillsdale, Michigan, 49242, January 1996, p. 2.

[3]Ibid., pp. 2, 4.

[4]Debbie Horton, used by permission.

[5]Dr. William Glasser, *Reality Therapy*, HarperCollins Publishers, 10 East 53rd St., New York, NY 10022, 1989.

[6]Luke Rader, "The Deadly Enemy of Christian Fellowship," *Reality*, Vol XXVII No. 6, P.O. Box 50, Washington, D.C. 20044, June, 2000, p. 1.

[7]Jon Courson, "Miriam, Aaron and the Green-Eyed Monster—Numbers 12," Tape #S3085, KAPL—Searchlight, Applegate Christian Fellowship, Jacksonville, OR, July 25-27, 2000.

[8]John Gottman, "New Ways to Tell If Your Love Will Last," *Glamour*, Feb. 1994, 203.2.

[9]Neil Clark Warren, Ph.D., *Learning To Live With The Love Of Your Life*, Tyndale House Publishers, Wheaton, Illinois, 1995, 147.

[10]Arthur Gordon, "How Wonderful You Are," *A Touch of Wonder—For People in Love with Life*, Fleming H. Revell, 1974, pp. 51-52.

[11]*"Cherished—Embracing Your First Love,"* Ibid.

Chapter 3

[1]Author unknown, Internet.

[2]Debbie Horton, used by permission

[3]For more on the subject of Jesus as our example of how to live, I refer you to the book *Become Like Jesus*. See page 132 for more information.

[4]*Webster's Ninth New Collegiate Dictionary,* 1989.

[5]Ibid.

[6]Ibid.

[7]Ibid.

[8]For more on how to forgive, see page 131 for information on Jack and Jeani Harroun's upcoming book, *The Path to Forgiveness.*

Chapter 4

[1]*Webster's,* Ibid.

[2]*Webster's,* Ibid.

[3]*Webster's,* Ibid.

[4]Mary Ruth Swope, Ph.D., *Bless Your Children Every Day,* Swope Enterprises, Inc. P.O. Box 62104, Phoenix, AZ 85082, p. 30.

[5]Ibid., p. 86.

Chapter 5

[1]Dr. Paul Coleman, *The 30 Secrets of Happily Married Couples,* p. 54.

[2]"Words That Hurt, Words That Heal: How To Choose Words Wisely And Well," Ibid., p. 1.

[3]Ibid., pp. 4, 5.

Appendix

SUGGESTED VERSES FOR MEDITATION AND MEMORIZATION

There are far more excellent Scripture verses than I am including here that one could commit to memory on the subject of our words, thoughts and heart. These are just a few to whet your appetite (the majority taken from the *New American Standard Bible*), in case you don't know where to begin. Even simply rereading these verses regularly and meditating on them would be good food for your spirit and mine. *We are what we eat.* That applies physically, but it also applies to our spirit life. If we ingest character-building truth regularly, it will show in our lives.

> **21 Death and life are in the power of the tongue. And those who love it will eat its fruit.**
> **—Proverbs 18**

> **29 Let no unwholesome word proceed from your mouth, but only such *a word* as is good for edification according to the need of *the moment*, that it may give grace to those who hear.**
> **—Ephesians 4**

34 ...For out of the abundance of the heart the mouth speaks.

—**Matthew 12,** *NKJV*

5 *We are* destroying speculations and every lofty thing raised up against the knowledge of God, and *we are* taking every thought captive to the obedience of Christ.

—**2 Corinthians 10**

23 Watch over your heart with all diligence,
   For from it *flow* the springs of life.
24 Put away from you a deceitful mouth,
   And put devious lips far from you.

—**Proverbs 4**

8 Finally, brethren, whatever is true, whatever is honorable, whatever is right, whatever is pure, whatever is lovely, whatever is of good repute, if there is any excellence and if anything worthy of praise, let your mind dwell on these things.

—**Philippians 4**

3 "The steadfast of mind Thou wilt keep in perfect peace,
   Because he trusts in Thee."

—**Isaiah 26**

5 For those who are according to the flesh set their minds on the things of the flesh, but those who are according to the Spirit, the things of the Spirit.
   6 For the mind set on the flesh is death, but the mind set on the Spirit is life and peace.

—**Romans 8**

36 "And I say to you, that every careless word that men shall speak, they shall render account for it in the day of judgment.

37 "For by your words you shall be justified, and by your words you shall be condemned."

—Matthew 12

16 Rejoice always;
17 pray without ceasing;
18 in everything give thanks; for this is God's will for you in Christ Jesus.

—1 Thessalonians 5

25 Anxiety in the heart of a man weighs it down,
But a good word makes it glad.

—Proverbs 12

23 The heart of the wise teaches his mouth,
And adds persuasiveness to his lips.
24 Pleasant words are a honeycomb,
Sweet to the soul and healing to the bones.

—Proverbs 16

3 Thou hast tried my heart;
Thou hast visited *me* by night;
Thou has tested me and dost find nothing;
I have purposed that my mouth will not transgress.

—Psalm 17

6 Let your speech always be with grace, seasoned, *as it were*, with salt, so that you may know how you should respond to each person.

—Colossians 4

3 Set a guard, O LORD, over my mouth;
Keep watch over the door of my lips.

—Psalm 141

14 Let the words of my mouth and the meditation
of my heart
Be acceptable in Thy sight, O LORD, my rock
and my redeemer.

—Psalm 19

And now may the Lord of peace Himself continually grant *you* peace in every circumstance (2 Thes. 3:16).

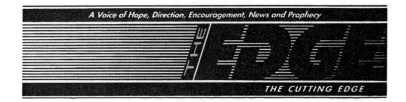

The Cutting Edge is a monthly Christian publication offering a *voice of hope, direction, and encouragement in the midst of troubled times.* You will gain a reputable resource that strongly advocates godly Christian values and highly esteems marriage and family, providing aids for healthier, happier relationships. This one-source, timely digest is *a watchman for you, alerting* you to items you might not otherwise see that pertain to you. That includes relevant news updates on world conditions and the church worldwide; key articles by Christian leaders that equip the saints for the work of the ministry (Ephesians 4:11-13), current perspectives on prophecy; articles to help you prepare for tough times and emergencies; and ways you can strengthen your immune system and physical health.

Through all of our publications, tapes, and videos, as well as the speaking ministry of Jack & Jeani Harroun, we seek to help the body of Christ to mature into the fullness of Christ, to be prepared spiritually, emotionally, and physically for the challenging future we are facing.

- -

The Cutting Edge Ministries   (541)826-9877
Jack & Jeani Harroun   Orders: (800)343-1111
P.O. Box 1788   E-mail: Edge@the-cutting-edge.org
Medford, OR 97501   Website: the-cutting-edge.org

ORDER FORM
AND
INFORMATION REQUEST

BC-131

Omega Publications   (541)826-4512
P.O. Box 4130   Fax (541)826-1023
Medford, OR 97501   EDGE@the-cutting-edge.org
                         http://the-cutting-edge.org

Please send me information on:

☐ *The Mighty Book Audio Book,* when available.

☐ *The Cutting Edge* monthly Christian news digest, edited by Jeani McKeever-Harroun *($30/year—Item #1921).*

☐ Jack and Jeani Harroun's upcoming books, when available, *Bridging the Gap (Between Men and Women)* and *The Path to Forgiveness.*

Please send me the following (payment enclosed):

☐ **Video(s)** by Jeani McKeever-Harroun *(Special: $17 each)*:
___ *Canning is Fun (#3851)*
___ *Dehydrating Made Easy (#3858)*
___ *A Practical Guide to Nutrition (#3856)*
___ *A Total Approach to Health (#3857)*

☐ Jeani's **music tape(s)** ($8 each):
___ *Jubilation*
___ *Wholly Holy*

Continued on next page

ORDER FORM

Continued from previous page

☐ I would like to order the following **books:**
____ More copies of *The Mighty Mouth* *($9–#2761)*
____ *Become Like Jesus ($10–#2200)*
Dr. James McKeever
____ *Bless Your Children Every Day,*
Dr. Mary Ruth Swope *($9–#2951)*
____ *Preparing For Emergencies ($12–#2225)*
Dr. James and Jeani McKeever
____ *Self-Reliant Living ($19–#2229)*
Dr. James and Jeani McKeever
____ *Self-Reliant Living Workbook ($49–#2231)*
Dr. James and Jeani McKeever

☐ Please send me the following:
____ *Cherished–Embracing Your First Love,* by Paul
Hegstrom, 2-Tape Audio Album *($12–#3028)*
____ *Unforgivable,* Emmy-nominated CBS Movie about
Paul and Judy Hegstrom's life *($29–#3976)*

NOTE: Please add $1.50 for shipping and handling for each book, video or music tape. Prices are subject to change.

Name _____

Address _____

City, State_____Zip_____
    Charge to: ☐ Visa ☐ Mastercard ☐ Discover

Card No. _____ Expires_____

Signature _____